Leopold von Berchtold

An Essay to Direct and Extend the Inquiries of Patriotic Travellers

With Further Observations on the Means of Preserving the Life, Health, and

Property of the Unexperienced in Their Journies by Land and Sea

Leopold von Berchtold

An Essay to Direct and Extend the Inquiries of Patriotic Travellers
With Further Observations on the Means of Preserving the Life, Health, and Property of the Unexperienced in Their Journies by Land and Sea

ISBN/EAN: 9783337309800

Printed in Europe, USA, Canada, Australia, Japan

Cover: Foto ©Andreas Hilbeck / pixelio.de

More available books at **www.hansebooks.com**

AN ESSAY

to direct and extend the Inquiries of

PATRIOTIC TRAVELLERS;

with further Observations on the Means of preserving the Life, Health, & Property of the unexperienced in their Journies by Land and Sea.

a Series of Questions, interesting to Society & Humanity, necessary to be proposed for Solution to Men of all Ranks & Employments, & of all Nations and Governments, comprising the most serious Points relative to the Objects of all Travels.

To which is Annexed

a List of English and foreign Works, intended for the Instruction and Benefit of Travellers, & a Catalogue of the most interesting European Travels, which have been published in different Languages, from the earliest Times, down to September 8th 1787.

By Count Leopold Berchtold,

Knight of the military Order of S.t Stephen of Tuscany &c. &c.

Inter studia versandum est, et inter auctores sapientiae; quamdiu nescieris, quid fugiendum, quid petendum, quid necessarium, quid supervacuum, quid justum, quid honestum, non erit hoc peregrinari, sed errare. — Seneca.

Vol. II.

LONDON.

Printed for the Author, and sold by M.r Robinson, M.r Debrett, M.r Payne, M.r Jeffery, & M.r Faulder.

1789.

Enter'd at Stationers Hall.

CONTENTS

OF

VOL. II.

A LIST of divers WORKS intended for the INSTRUCTION of TRAVELLERS.
Page 1

A CATALOGUE of the moſt intereſting EUROPEAN TRAVELS.

	Page		Page
Adriatic Sea,	14	Aſſow, (the Sea of)	25
Ætna (Mount)	15	Aſturias, - - -	25
Aland, - - -	16	Athens, - - -	25
Alps, - - -	16	Athos, (Mount)	25
Alſace, - - -	18	Auvergne, - -	26
Altai Mountains in		Aunis, - - -	26
Siberia, - -	19	Auſtria, - - -	26
Altdorf, - - -	19	Baltic Sea, - -	28
Amſterdam, -	20	Bareith, - - -	29
Angleſey, - -	20	Barrois, - - -	29
Angermanland, or		Barcelona, - -	29
Angermania, -	21	Baſil, - - -	29
Angoumois, - -	21	Bavaria, - - -	30
Antrim, - - -	21	Beaujolois, - -	31
Appenzell, - -	22	Bedfordſhire, - -	32
Archangel, - -	22	Belgrad, - - -	32
Archipelago, -	22	Bellentz, - -	32
		Belluno	

CONTENTS.

	Page		Page
Belluno,	32	Cherfo in the Adriat.	46
Bergamo,	33	Chefhire,	46
Berlin,	33	Cloud, (Saint)	47
Black Sea,	34	Cologne,	47
Blanc, (Mount)	34	Compoftella,	47
Blankenburgh,	35	Conftance,	47
Blockfberg,	35	Conftantinople,	48
Bohemia,	35	Copenhagen,	54
Bofphorus of Thrace,	37	Corfu,	55
		Cork,	55
Bothnia,	37	Cornwall,	55
Brabant,	37	Corfica,	55
Brandenburgh,	38	Courland,	57
Bremen,	39	Crim,	58
Brefcia,	40	Croatia,	59
Brunfwick,	40	Cumberland,	60
Bruffels,	40	Cyprus,	60
Buckingham,	40	Czirknitz (Lake of)	61
Bulgaria,	40	Dalmatia,	61
Cadix,	41	Danube river,	63
Canary Iflands,	41	Dauphiné,	64
Candia,	43	Denmark,	64
Carinthia,	43	Derbyfhire,	70
Carniola,	44	Devonfhire,	70
Caffel,	44	Dorfetfhire,	70
Catalonia,	45	Drefden,	70
Cefalonia,	45	Dublin,	71
Champaign,	45	Durham,	71
Chantilly,	46	Edinburgh,	71
		Eifenach,	

CONTENTS.

	Page		Page
Fifenach,	72	Greenland,	138
Elba,	72	Grifons, Country	
England,	72	of the	142
Erini, (Saint)	90	Guernfey,	142
Ermenonville,	90	Hague,	143
Europe,	90	Hamburgh,	143
Ferro Iflands,	103	Hanover,	143
Ferney,	104	Hertfordfhire,	143
Fichtelberg,	104	Harwich,	143
Finland,	105	Harz,	144
Flanders,	106	Hebrides,	145
Forez,	107	Hermanftadt,	146
Formentera,	107	Herrnhut,	146
Franche Comté,	108	Hefle,	146
France,	108	Holland,	147
Franconia,	122	Holftein,	151
Friuli,	122	Hungary,	151
Geneva,	122	Icy Sea,	153
Genoa,	123	Iceland,	153
Germany,	123	Ireland,	156
Gibraltar,	132	Iftria,	158
Glaris,	133	Italy,	158
Gloucefterfhire,	132	Jutland,	171
Glockner Mountain, in Tyrol,	134	Kent,	171
		Kerry,	171
Gotha,	134	Kiel,	171
Gothland,	134	Kilda, St.	172
St. Gothard (Mt.)	135	Kilia Nova,	172
Greece,	135	Kupferberghen,	172
			Lancafhire

CONTENTS.

	Page		Page
Lancashire,	172	Majorca, - -	183
Languedoc, - -	172	Malaga, - -	183
Lapland, - -	173	Malta, - - -	184
Lavis, - - -	175	Man (Isle of) -	185
Lausanne, - -	175	Mantua, - -	185
Leicester, - -	175	Marburg, - -	185
Lemberg, - -	175	Marly, - - -	186
Leipzic, - - -	175	Maura, (St.) - -	186
Leyden, - - -	176	Mecklenburg, -	186
Liege, - - -	176	Mediterranean Sea,	186
Lippari Islands,	176	Mentz, - - -	187
Lisbon, - - -	177	Middlesex, - -	187
Lithuania, - -	177	Milan, - -	187
Lithuania, (Prus.)	178	Minden, - -	188
Livinerthal, -	178	Minorca, - -	188
Livonia, - -	178	Moldavia, - -	188
Lombardy, - -	179	Monmouthshire,	189
London, - -	179	Moravia, - -	189
Loretto, - -	180	Morea, - - -	190
Lorrain, - -	180	Munich, - -	191
Lubeck, - -	181	Naples, - -	191
Lucern, (Lake of)	181	Nassau, - - -	192
Lusatia, - -	181	Negropont, - -	193
Luxemburg, -	182	Netherlands, -	193
Lyonnois, - -	182	Neufchatel, - -	196
Macedonia, - -	182	Nicaria, - - -	197
Madeira, - -	182	Norfolk, - -	197
Madrid, - -	183	Normandy, -	197
Magdeburg, -	183	Northern Countries	197
		Northamptonshire	

CONTENTS.

	Page		Page
Northamptonshire,	201	Pyrenean Mountains,	216
North Sea,	201	Ragusa,	216
Northumberland,	201	Rhine Countries,	217
Norway,	202	Rhodus,	217
Nottinghamshire,	203	Riesengeburg,	218
Nova Zembla,	203	Riga,	218
Oland,	203	Rome,	218
Orenburg,	204	Romania,	220
Orkney Islands,	204	Ronca,	220
Oxfordshire,	205	Russia,	221
Padua,	205	Saltzburg,	229
Palatinate,	205	Samos,	229
Paris,	205	Sardinia,	229
Passau,	207	Savoy,	230
Patmos,	207	Saxony,	230
Peloponesus,	207	Schafhausen,	231
Petersburg,	207	The Schwartzwald or Black Forest,	231
Piedmont,	208		
Pilate (Mount of)	208	Scilly Islands,	231
Pistoja,	208	Scio,	232
Poland,	209	Sclavonia,	232
Pomerania,	210	Scotland,	232
Pope's Dominions,	211	Servia,	235
Portugal,	211	Shetland Islands,	235
Potsdam,	214	Sicily,	235
Prague,	214	Sierra Morena,	237
Presburg,	214	Silesia,	237
Provence,	214	Simenthal,	238
Prussia,	215		Sleswick

CONTENTS.

	Page		Page
Slefwick,	238	Turkey,	261
Spain,	238	Tufcany,	268
Spaw,	244	Ukraine,	268
Spitfbergen,	244	Upland,	269
Staffordfhire,	244	Vallengin,	269
Stiria,	245	Velai,	269
Stirlingfhire,	245	Venice,	269
Stockholm,	246	Verfailles,	270
Strait Davis,	246	Vefuvius,	270
Strafburgh,	246	Vienna,	272
Surrey,	246	Wallachia,	272
Suffex,	247	Wales,	273
Swabia,	247	Warwickfhire,	274
Sweden,	248	Waterford,	274
Switzerland,	250	Waygats Straits,	274
Tartary,	257	Weimar,	274
Temefvar,	259	Weftmoreland,	275
Teneriffe,	259	Weftphalia,	275
Theffaly,	259	Wight (Ifle of)	275
Thracia,	259	Wurtemberg,	276
Tirol,	260	Yorkfhire,	279
Tranfylvania,	260	Yviça,	276
Triefte,	260	Zante,	276
Turin,	261	Zurch, Lake of	276

CON-

CONTENTS

OF THE

APPENDIX

TO THE

LIST OF WORKS,

INTENDED FOR

The Inſtruction and Benefit of Travellers.

Page 277

CONTENTS

Of the APPENDIX to the EUROPEAN TRAVELS

	Page		Page
Archipelago,	278	Germany, -	279
Auſtria, - -	278	Hungary, - -	280
Bannat of Temeſ-war, - -	278	Minorca, -	280
		Norway, - -	280
Burgundy, -	278	Ruſſia, - - -	280
England, - -	279	Saxony, - -	281
Frieſland, - -	279	Tuſcany, - -	281

ERRATA.

The Author begs leave to inform the intelligent reader, that he did not think himself entitled to make any alteration whatever in the Orthography of the titles of the ancient writers contained in this Catalogue; therefore he hopes the deviations from the present manner of spelling will not be looked upon as proofs of his want of knowledge of the modern way of writing, or of his carelesness in correcting.

Errata which have happened in the Press, such as the misplacing, changing, adding or omitting a letter, &c. &c. as they make no alteration in the sense, will easily be excused by all generous readers, who have a competent knowledge of the difficulties attending the printing of a work of this nature.

Page 17, line 27, *for* De Ben,   *read* Ben de.
— 23, — 25, — Conta,   — Conte.
— 38, — 1, — de,   — du.
— ib. — 3, — II,   — IV.
— 40, laſt line — Boſſano,   — Baſſano.
— 42, — 26, — Nun'ez de Peñ'a, — Nuñez de Peña.
— 49, — 26, — Daes(Jovis von der) — Does (Joris van der)
— 50, — 27, — 1vo.   — 8vo.
— 54, — 4, — Troil,   — Troilo
— 67, — 27, — Allius,   — Cellius
— 97, — 4, — Montague,(L.M.W.) *add* Letters during her travels in Europe, &c.
— 109, — 6, *after* en,   *add* 1774, 1775, Berlin.
— 114, — 18, *for* Lemhard,   *read* Leonhard.
— 118, — 6, *after* London,   *insert* 1673.
— ib. — 8, *for* 1763,   *read* 1673.

ERRATA.

Page 137, line 14, *for* 1781,   *read* 1731.
— ib. — 15, *after* Amſt, 1733, 8vo.   *insert* 4 tom. A Paris, 1739, 4to.
— 140, — 19, — 1653,   — A Paris, 1672, 1676,
— 141, — 6, — Paris,   — 1643, 1647, 8vo. A Amſterd.
— 145, — 24, *for* Hebrdes,   *read* Hebrides.
— 150, — 19, — Spoert's   — Spoerl's.
— 154, — 15, — 1683,   — 1753.
— ib. — 28, — Sorve,   — Soroe.
— 160, — 3, — 1782,   — 1723.
— 170, laſt line — 3to.   — 4to.
— 174, — 6, — 1767, 4to.   — 1771, 8vo.
— 195, — 5, — 1689,   — 1769.
— 196, — 22, *after* Vallengin,   — à Neufchatel
— 204, — 21, *for* Malo.   — Malgo,
— 205, — 14, — Anzeige,   — Aufzüge.
— 206, — 16, — portative.   — portatif.
— 207, — 1 — 1783,   — 1782.
— 214, — 15, — Lahman,   — Lehman,
— 226, — 14, *after* Moſcovia,   *add* Wilnae, 1586, 8vo.
— 237, — 17, *for* Hammond,   *read* Hammard
— 238, — 5, — Slewick,   — Sleſwick.
— 243, — 24, — Murr,   — by Murck.
— 252, — 17, — 1757,   — 1775.
— 258, — 7, *to* regionibus,   *add* Orientalibus.
— ib. — 25, *before* Zeiten,   *omit* bewährteſten.

LIST OF DIVERS WORKS

INTENDED FOR THE INSTRUCTION OF

TRAVELLERS.

IN ENGLISH.

AGREEMENTS of the cuftoms of the Indians and Jews, with inftructions for travellers, 8vo.

A common place-book for travellers.

ANDREWS's (JOHN) letters to a young gentleman on his fetting out for France; with rules and directions for travellers, and various anecdotes relating to the fubject. London, 1784.

Bear-leaders or modern travelling, 8vo.

BOWLES's Poft Chaife Companion, 2 vol. 12mo. London.

Ditto Britannia Depicta, London.

A   Companion

Companion for all gentlemen travellers and traders. London, 1709, 8vo.

Dr. TUCKER's inftructions for travellers, 1757, 4to.

Dialogues on the ufe of foreign travels. London, 1764, 8vo.

GRANTHAM on travels, 12mo.

HOWELL's inftructions for travellers, 1650.

KITCHEN's Poft Chaife Companion, London.

LEIGH's (EDWARD) three Diatribes: or Difcourfes of travel, of money, or coins, of meafuring of the diftance betwixt place and place. London, 1671, 8vo.

LETTSOM's (JOHN COAKLEY) Naturalifts and Traveller's Companion, 8vo.

Letters to a young nobleman on travels, 12mo.

LASSEL's defcription of Italy, with inftructions for travellers, 1660.

Letter of advice to a young gentleman on his travels, London, 1788, 8vo.

NELSON's inftructions for foreign travels, 1718, 12mo.

Profitable inftructions defcribing what fpecial obfervations are to be taken by travellers, by the three much admired ftatefmen, ROBERT EARL OF ESSEX, SIR PHILIP SIDNEY, AND SECRETARY DAVISON. London, 1633.

PATTERSON's travelling dictionary, 8vo. 2 vol.

The infallible guide to travellers, by W. H. London, 1682, 8vo

Thoughts on ancient and modern travels, 8vo.

Traveller's pocket Book.

TURLERUS (HIERONIMUS) the traveller. London, 1575, 12mo.

IN FOREIGN LANGUAGES.

AUCTORES varii de arte peregrinandi. Norimb. 1591, 12mo.

Allgemeines Europeifches Poft und Reife Buch, nebft Anzeige aller in Europa gangbaren Müntz-Sorten. Gewichte, und Ellen-Maffen. Prefburg, 1783, 8vo.

BARTHOLINUS (THOM.) de peregrinatione medica tractatus. Hafniae, 1674, 4to.

BAUDELOT DE DAIRVAL de l'utilité des voyages, & de l'avantage, que la recherche des antiquités procure aux fçavans. A Paris, 1686. gr. 12mo. II tomes.

Do. A Paris, 1693. gr. 12mo.

Do. A Rouen, 1727. 8vo. II tomes.

BELLEGARDE (JEAN BAPT. MORRAN ABBE DE) hiftoire univerfelle des voyages par mer, & par terre, dans l'ancien, & le nouveau monde; avec un difcours preliminaire fur l'utilité des voyages.

A Paris,

A Paris, 1707. gr. 12mo.

Do. A Amsterdam, 1758. gr. 12mo.

BERGER (THEOD) de prudentia apodemica. Lips. 1712, 4to.

BERNEGGERI (MATTH.) discursus historico-politicus, seu dissertatio de peregrinationibus studioforum. Argent. 1619, 4to.

BESPLAS de l'utilité des voyages.

BUDDEI (JOH. FRANC) dissertatio historica de peregrinationibus Pythagoræ. Jenæ, 1692, 4to.

COLERUS (Jo. CHRISTOPH.) de illustribus principum juventutis peregrinationibus. Witt. 1714, 4to.

CONRINGI (HERM.) de prudentia peregrinandi disquisitio politica. Helmst. 1663, 4to.

Do. Helmst. 1677, 4to.

Crausii (RUD. WILP.) programma de peregrinationibus Germanorum, medicae artis studioforum. Jenae, 1704, 4to.

DIETERICUS (Jo. CONR.) de peregrinatione studioforum. Marp. 1640, 4to.

DOPPERTI (Jo.) spicilegium de prisci ac medii aevi itineribus, doctrinae locupletandae causa susceptis. Sneebergae, 1712, 4to.

De arte peregrinandi collectio. Lips. 1691. 12mo.

Discours sur l'utilité des voyages. A Naples, 1780, 4to.

Der wohlerfahrne Wandersman. Frankf. 1692, 8vo.

Des wohlerfahrnen Wandersmans erſte Fortſetzung. Frankf. 1695, 8vo.

Die rechte Reiſekunſt oder Anleitung, wie eine Reiſe in die Fremde, ſonderlich nach Frankreich anzuſtellen. Frankfurt, 1674, 12mo.

Der Reiſende: ein Wochenblatt zur Aufbreitung gemein-nutziger Kántnüſſe. Hamb. 1782, 8vo.

ENGEL (MAURIT.) Diſſertatio politica de prudentia peregrinandi. Viteb. 1689, 4to.

Extraits des difcours, qui ont concouru pour le prix, que l'academie des ſciences de Lyon a adjugé à Monſr. Turlin avocat au parlement de Paris ſur cette queſtion: Les voyages peuvent ils être conſiderés comme un moyen à perfectionner l'education. A Lyon, 1788. 8vo.

FOUR (SYLV. DU) Inſtruction morale d'un pere à ſon fils, qui part pour un long voyage. A Geneve, 1676, 8vo.

FRANCI (NIC. BARTH.) exercitatio academica de peregrinatione veterum ſapientum, eruditionis ergo ſuſcepta. Lips. 1679, 4to.

FROELICH (DAN.) bibliotheca peregrinantium ſeu viatorum. Ulmae, 1643, 12mo. II tom.

FURSTENHOLD (EUSEBII) examen judicii de Conſtantini Germanici itinerario politico, 1670, 12mo.

Fremder og Reiſender Hand Lexicon. Kiob. 1780, 8vo.

GAUDENTIO (SAGANINO) della peregrinazione filoſophica trattatello con una aggiunta geografica. In Piſa, 1643, 4to.

GIRALDI (LILII GREGOR.) de navigiis & navigationibus, ſeu de re nautica libellus. Basileae, 1540, 8vo.

GOTTSCHED (JOH. CHRIST.) ſingularia Vindobonenſia. Praemittitur praclufio, itineris litterarii rationem reddens. Lips. 1750, 4to.

GRATAROLUS (GUIL.) de regimine iter agentium, vel equitum, vel peditum, vel navi, vel curru ſeu rheda. Baſil. 1561. 12mo.

GRILLO (Jo. DAR.) oratio de peregrinationibus litterariis in academiis recte inſtituendis. Francof. ad Viad. 1727, 4to.

Gedanken über Reiſen: nebſt allgemeinen Anmerkungen, wie man ſolche nutzlich anwenden könne. Frankfurt, 1781, 8vo.

GUINDERODE (FRIED. JUST. FREYHERR VON) Gedanken über Reiſen, nebſt allgemeiner Anweiſung, wie man ſolche nutzlich anſtellen könne. Frankfurt, 1781, 8vo.

Guia

Guia de caminos para ir por todas las provincias de España, Francia, Italia, y Alemania. En Madrid, 1705, 12mo.

HALL (Jos.) quo vadis? ou cenfures des voyages entrepris par les Seigneurs & les Gentilfhommes, traduites de l'Anglois, par Jacquemot, A Geneve, 1628.

HENNERS (JOH.) Politifcher Difcours de arte apodemica, & vera peregrinandi ratione. Tubing. 1609, 12mo.

HESSI (EOBANI) de profectione ad Des. Erafmum hodoeporicum. Erf. 1518, 4to.

HORNII (GEORG.) Ulyffea, feu ftudiofus peregrinans. Franc. & Lips, 1672, 12mo.

HORNING (REINHOLD) de peregrinationibus, utrum litterariis prodeffe queant, necne? Regiom, 1725, 4to.

HOVNOVII (MICH.) differtatio politica de peregrinatione. Refp. & auctore Abrah. Everbeck. Regiom, 1691, 4to.

Handbuch für Reifende aus allen Ständen. Leipzig, 1784, 8vo.

Hermes politicus, five de peregrinatoria prudentia. Francof, 1608, 12mo.

HAEFFELIN (CASIM) difcours des influences des voyages fur le progrès des arts, &c. Manheim, 1775, 4to.

HURD—von dem Nutzen der Reifen in fremde Länder, in einer Unterredung zwifchen dem Lord Shaftefbury and Mr.
John

John Locke: Aus dem Englischen von C. H. Wilken. Breslau, 1765.

Ditto, unter Hurd's Nahmen Unterhaltungen über die ausländischen Reisen in Ruckficht der Erziehung. Leipzig, 1777. 8vo.

JACOBS (FRID. HENR.) de peregrinationum eruditarum ortu, progreffu, & fine. Jenae, 1705, 4to.

JORDAN (P. SIMON) von dem Nutzen der Reifen; unter dem Nahmen verfchiedenes zum lefen von Mr. Raodin. Augfburg, 1768.

Judicium de Conftantini Germanici itinerario politico, 1669, 12mo.

Itineraire des routes les plus frequentées. Paris, 1775, 8vo.

KRIEGK (GEORG. NIC.) de peregrinationibus Romanorum academicis. Jenae, 1704, 4to.

LETTSOM (JOHN COAKLEY) voyageur naturalifte, ou inftruction fur les moyens de ramaffer les objets de l'hiftoire naturelle & de les bien conferver. A Amfterdam, 1775, 12mo.

LINNAEI (CAR,) oratio de neceffitate peregrinationum intra patriam.

LOESCHER (JOH. CASP.) de peregrinationibus litterariis. Witt. 1697, 4to.

LOYSII

LOYSII (GEORG.) privilegium Mercurii, feu de praeftantiflimis peregrinantium virtutibus. Spirae, 1601, 2mo.

L'art de voyager utilement. A Amft. 1698, 12mo.

Lehrreiche Nachrichten für Reifende. Berlin, 1738, 8vo. II Theile.

Le voyageur philofophe, 2 tom. A Amfterdam, 1761.

La vera guida per chi viaggia, con la defcrizione delle 4 pàrti del mondo, 16mo. In Roma, 1771.

LINNE (CAR. A) inftructio peregrinatoris. Upfal. 1759, 4to.

Do. Lugd. Bat. 1762, 8vo.

Le flambeau des voyageurs. A Utrecht, 1765.

MARPERGERS (PAUL JACOB) kluger und vorsichtiger Paffagier, oder Unterricht, welchergeftalt Reifende ihre Reifen zu Waffer und zu Lande klug anftellen mögen. Chemnitz, 1707, 12mo.

MARPERGER (PAUL JACOB) der feinem Stande und Profeffion nach wohl unterwiefene Paffagier. Drefden, 1723, 8vo.

MEIENSTRAND (A) methodus apodemica. Lips. 1588, 12mo.

MEYERI (ALB.) methodus apodemica. Roftock, 1591, 8vo.

MURALT, Lettres fur les Anglois, & les François, & fur les voyages, 1725, 8vo.

B   Do

Do. 1728.

Methodo apodemico de viajar, en Latin por el P. Don Oliver Legipont Aleman, de la orden de San Benito; y traducido en Efpañol por el Doctor Joaquin Marin. Ao. 1759, en Valencia.

NEMEITZ (JOH. CHR.) (anfänglich unter dem Nahmen Timentes) Sejour de Paris, oder Anleitung, wie Reifende von Condition fich zu verhalten haben, wenn fie ihre Zeit und Geld wohl zu Paris anwenden wollen. Frankf. 1718, 1722, 8vo. Strafb. 1780, 8vo.

------- Sejour de Paris, ou inftruction pour les voyageurs de condition, s'ils veulent faire un bon ufage de leur tems & argent duant leur fejour à Paris. A Leide, 1727. 8vo. II tom.

OLDENBURGERI (PHIL. ANDR.) (fubnomine Conftantini Germanici) epiftola politica ad Juftinum Sincerum de peregrinationibus Germanorum recte inftituendis, in qua depinguntur Germaniae Principum mores, doctrina, inclinationes, vota, fpes, & metus, &c. Cofmopoli, 1669, 12mo.

PITSIUS (JO.) de peregrinatione. Duffeld. 1601, 12mo,

PYRCKMEIER (HILARIUS) de arte peregrinandi, 1591, 12mo.

Pere-

Peregrinandi ars, &c. Norimbergae, 1591.

Ranzovii (Henr.) methodus apodemica, feu peregrinandi, perluftrandique urbes, & regiones ratio, cum Loysii (Georg.) privilegio Mercurii. Argent. 1608, 12mo.

Reife und Kauffmanns Almanach. Hamburg, 1782, 8vo.

Reifen in Rucksicht der Erziehung. Leipzig, 1777.

Reichard's (Heinrich Chr.) Hand-Buch für Reifende aus allen Ständen. Leipzig, 1785. gr. 8vo. mit 3 Karten.

Sanden de peregrinatione medici. Regiom, 1725, 4to.

Schefelii (Christ. Steph.) programma de peregrinationibus Philiàtrorum, earumque utilitate Griphifw. 1730, 4to.

Schoening (Godof.) de peregrinatione, auctore & refpondente Joh. Hardero. Viteb. 1697, 4to.

Schlözer's (A. L.) Entwurf zu einem Reife Collegium. Götting. 1777. 8vo.

Senstii (Joh. Chr.) differtatio de peregrinatione docta rite inftituenda. Roft. 1716, 4to.

Stockharti (Gottl.) idea ftudiofi peregrinantis. Lipfiae, 1688, 4to.

Saggio per fervire alla ftoria de'viaggi filofofici, e dei prencipi viaggiatori. In Venezia, 1780, 8vo.

SCHLEGEL's (GOTTL.) Chriftliche Betrachtungen auf Reifen. Riga, 1782, 8vo.

SPRENGEL's (M. C.) Gefchichte der wichtigften geographifchen Entdeckungen durch Reifen. Hall. 1783, 8vo.

SCHORART's (AUG. WILH.) thefaurus peregrinantium, oder Anweifung, wie ein Reifender fremde Länder eigentlich betrachten foll. Frankf. an der Oder, 1708. 8vo.

THOMASII (JENKIN) oratio de peregrinationis litterariae infigni utilitate. Bafil. 1707, 4to.

TIMMII (Jo) Ulyffes Germanicus, oder vernunftmäffige Abhandlung der von Teutfchen anzuftellenden Reifen. Bremen, 1734, 8vo.

Voyage de la raifon en Europe, 1772.

Verhaltungs Regeln für unerfahrne Reifende zu Pferd. Gera, 1783, 8vo.

VEDARI, il viaggio in prattica per chi vuol viaggiare per tutte le ftrade e pofte d'Europa. In Venezia, 1742, 12mo.

WEIGEL's neu erfundener Reife-Rath. Jena 1674, 4to.

WILLI (JOH. VALENT) fub nomine (Joach. Viti) Wigand differtationes tres de Philiatrorum Germanorum itineribus. Friburgi & Francof. 1678, 12mo.

WILLEBRAND's (JOH. PETR.) hiftorifche Berichte und praktifche Anmerkungen auf Reifen

Reifen in Deutfchland, und andern Ländern. Hamburg, 1758, 8vo. Frankf. & Leipz. 1758. gr. 8vo. Leipz. 1769.

WINCKLERI, de prudentia apodemica, Vit. 1720, 4to.

ZAMELII (GODOF.) ftudiofus apodemicus, feu de peregrinatione ftudioforum. Bremae, 1651, 12mo.

ZENTGRAVII (JOH. JOACH.) differtatio de peregrinatione apodemica.

ZWINGERI (THEOD.) methodus apodemica in gratiam eorum, qui in quocumque vitae genere peregrinari cupiunt. Bafil. 1577, 4to. Argent, 1594, 4to.

ZOBEL's (ERN FRID.) Neu eingerichtetes Hand und Reifebuch. Altdorff, 1755. 8vo. Altd. 1774, 8vo.

A CATALOGUE

OF THE MOST INTERESTING

EUROPEAN TRAVELS

Which have been published in different Languages

From the earliest Times down to Sept. 8th. 1787.

ADRIATIC SEA.

DONATI (VITALIANO) Saggio della storia naturale marina dell'Adriatico, con lettera del Sigr. Leonardo Sesler intorno ad un nuovo genere di piante terrestri. In Venez. 1750, 4to.

The same work has been published in German. Hall, 1753, 4to.

Ditto in French. A la Haye, 1758, 4to.

SPALANZANI (ABBATE) Lettere al Sigr. Marchese Lucchesini di suo viaggio attorno le coste dell' Adriatico. In Pavia, 1783, 4to. IV vol.

ÆTNA

ÆTNA MOUNT.

BEMBI (PET.) de Aetna ad Gabrielem liber. Venet. 1495, 4to.
Do. Venet. 1530, 4to. Lugd. 1552, 8vo.
CARRERA (PIETRO) il Mongibello. In Catania, 1636, 4to.
HAMILTON'S (SIR WM.) Observations on Mount Vesuvius, Mount Aetna, and other Volcanos, in a series of Letters. London, 1772, 8vo.
Ditto in German. Berlin, 1773, 8vo.
Do. Bericht vom gegenwärtigen Zustand des Vesuvs, und Beschreibung einer Reise in die Provinz Abruzzo, und nach der Insul Ponza. Dresden, 1787, 8vo.
HAMILTON'S (SIR WM.) Campi Phlegrei: Observations on the Volcanos of the two Sicilies, &c.
Observations sur les Volcans des deux Siciles, &c. A Naples, 1776. gr. fol. II tom.
------ oeuvres complettes du Vesuve & de l'Etna commentées par MR. L'ABBE GIRAUD SOULAVIE. A Paris, 1781, 8vo.
HOMODEIS (ANT. PHILOTHEI DE) Aetnae topographia, incendiorumque Aetneorum historia

hiftoria; ex editione Nic. Oddi. Venet. 1591, 4to.

SEVERUS (PUBL. CORNEL.) Etna, überfezt von C. A. Schmid. Braunfchw. 1769, 8vo.

A L A N D.

RUDBECK's (OLOF) Nora Smoland eller uplyfte Lapland & Rudbeckii filii (Olai) Lapponia illuftrata, & iter per Uplandiam, Angermanniam, Bothniam, item Finlandiam, Alandiam, &c. Upfaliae, 1701, 4to.

A L P S.

BOURRIT (M. TH.) nouvelle defcription des Glacieres de Savoye, particulierement de la vallée de Chamouni, & du Mont Blanc. A Geneve, 1785, 8vo.

------ Befchreibung der Savoifchen Eifgebürge oder Fortfetzung der Befchreibung der Penninifchen und Rhaetifchen Alpen. Zürch, 1786, 8vo.

BOURRIT (MARC. THEOD.) Voyage pittorefque aux glacieres de Savoye en 1772. *Ditto.* A Geneve, 1773. 12mo.

Ditto

Ditto in German. Nurnberg, 1775, 8vo. & Gotha, 1775, 8vo.
Ditto in Dutch. t'Amsterdam, 1779. gr. 8vo.
Do. Description des Alpes Pennines & Rhetiennes. A Geneve, 1781. 8vo. II tom.
Ditto in German. Zurch, 1782, 8vo.
CONTURBIO (GIO.) Descrizione delle Alpi, che dividono l'Italia dalla Germania, e dalla Francia, con i paſſi, per dove poſſono condurſi eferciti. In Milano, 1620, 4to.
HACQUET's (B.) Phyſicaliſch-politiſche Reiſen aus den Dinariſchen, durch die Juliſchen, Carniſchen und Rhaetiſchen in die Noriſchen Alpen in den Jahren, 1781, und 1783. Leipzig, 1785. gr. 8vo. 2 Th.
LUC (JEAN AND. DE) Relation de differens voyages dans les Alpes de Faucigny, avec les annotations du traduƈteur. A Maſtricht, 1776, 8vo.
Ditto in German, Bern, 1775. *gr.* 8vo. *Leipzig,* 1777, 8vo.
NERINI (F. M.) Iter Subalpinum, cura (J. C.) Fiſcheri. Francof. & Lipſiae, 1754, 8vo.
SAUSSURE (HORACE DE BEN.) Voyages dans les Alpes, precedés d'un eſſai ſur l'hiſtoire naturelle des environs de Geneve. A Neufchatel, 1779, gr. 4to.

C   Do.

Do. A Geneve, 1780, gr. 8vo. II tom. A.
Geneve, 1786. gr. 8vo. Tom. III. & IV
Ditto in German. Leipzig, 1781. gr. 8vo. *II
Th.* Leipzig, 1787, 3 *Th.*
SIMLERI (JOSUAE) Vallefiae defcriptio Libri
II. & de Alpibus commentarius, & Collini
(Cafp.) liber de thermis & fontibus medicatis Vallefianorum. Tigur. 1574, 8vo.
Sub titulo Vallefiae & Alpum defcriptio.
Lugd. Batavorum, 1633, 24mo.
STORR's (GOTTL. CONR. CHRIST.) Alpenreife im Jahr. 1781. Leipzig, 1784, 1786,
4to. II Th.

ALSACE.

BREVAL's (JOHN) remarks on feveral parts
of Europe, relating chiefly to the hiftory, antiquities, and geography of France,
Low Countries, Lorrain, Germany, Savoy, Tyrol, Switzerland, Italy, and Spain.
London, 1726. Fol. II vol.
HUNCZOWSKY (J.) medicinifch chirurgifche
Bemerkungen auf feinen Reifen durch
Elfas, und den Weftlichen und Sudlichen
Theil von Frankreich, befonders über die
Hofpitäler. Wien. 1783, 8vo.
M. (C. D. S.) nouveau voyage de la
Grece, d'Egypte, de Palcftine, d'Italie,

de

de Suisse, d' Alsace, & des Païs Bas fait en 1721, 1723. A la Haye, 1724, 12mo.
Ditto in English, London, 1725, 8vo.
Ditto 1738, 8vo.
POCOCKE (RICH.) vide ARCHIPELAGO.
SULZER's (FR. JOS.) litterarifche Reife durch Siebenburgen, Ungarn, Oefterreich, Bayern, Bannat, Schwaben, Schweitz, Elfas, &c. 1782, 8vo.
Vues pittoresques de l'Alsace deffinées, gravées, & terminées en biftre par MONSR. WALTER, citoyen de Strafbourg; accompagnées d'un texte hiftorique par MR. L' ABBE GRANDIDIER, hiftoriographe du Roi en Alsace. A Strafburg, 1785, fo.

ALTAI MOUNTAINS IN SIBERIA.

PATRIN, relation d'un voyage aux monts d' Altai en Siberie, pendant l'année 1781. A. St. Peterfb. 1783, gr. 8vo.

ALTDORF.

WILL's (GEO. ANDR.) Briefe über eine Reife nach Sachfen von Altdorf über Bareuth in das Erzgebürge. Altdorf, 1785, 8vo.

AMSTER-

AMSTERDAM.

ADLER's (JO. GEORG. CHRIST.) kurzgefaſte Uberſicht ſeiner in den Jahren, 1780, 1782, über Wienn, Venedig, und Rom, und von dort uber Mayland, Turin, Paris, Amſterdam, und Leiden zur Critic der Bibel, in Durchſuchung alter Handſchriſten gethanen Reiſe. Altona, 1783, 8vo.

PIGNATA (JOSEPH) avantures avec ſon voyage de Rome à Amſterdám. A Cologne, 1725, 8vo.

VOLCKARD's (ADR. GOTTL.) Reiſen und Schiffahrten durch Nieder Sachſen nach Hamburg und Amſterdam; von da nach Cadix, Gibraltar, Neapolis, Smyrna, und weiter in Norden bis Archangel, &c. Budiſſin, 1735, 8vo.

ANGLESEY.

A Hiſtory of the Iſland of Angleſey. Lond. 1775, 4to.

HACKLUYT's (RICHARD) principal navigations, voyages,

voyages, &c. of the English nation. London, 1600, fol. 2 vol.

ROWLAND's (HENRY) Mona antiqua. Dublin, 1723, 4to.

ANGERMANLAND.

GISLER (NILS) tal om Medelpads och Angermanlands naturlige lynne och Beskaffenhet. Stockh. 1751, 8vo.

RUDBECK's (OLOF.) vide ALAND.

ANGOUMOIS.

MEUNIER (DE) essai d' une methode generale propre à étendre les connoissances des voyageurs, (dans l'Angoumois). A Paris, 1779, 8vo. 2 vol.

ANTRIM.

HAMILTON's (SIR WILL.) Letters concerning the Northern coast of Antrim, in Ireland. London, 1786, 8vo.

APPENZELL.

AISPRUNG's (JOH. MICH.) Reife von Ulm nach St. Gallen, Appenzell, Glaris, Uri, Schweitz, Zug, und Zurch bis Coftnitz in Briefen. Leipzig, 1784, 8vo.

ARCHANGEL.

ALLISON's (THOM.) Account of a voyage from Archangel in Ruffia, in the year 1696. London, 1699, 8vo.

VOLCKARD (ADR. GOTTL.) *vide* AMSTERDAM.

ARCHIPELAGO.

BLAINVILLE's (VON) Reifebefchreibung durch Holland, Deutfchland, Schweitz, Italien, Frankreich, Griechifche Infeln, &c. uberfetzt aus den Englifchen, mit Anmerkungen von Koehler, Lemgo, 1764, 1766, 1767, gr. 4to. V. Bände.

BLANC (VINCENT LE) Voyage aux quatre parties du monde. A Paris, 1649, 4to. Troyes, 1658, 4to.

Ditto, Verdeelung der 48 jaarigen reifen door

door Europa, Afia, Africa, en America. Amfterdam, 1654.

DAPPER (OLIFER) naaukeurige befchryving der eylanden in de Archipel der Middellandfche zee; t' Amfterdam, 1688, fo.

Ditto, in French. A Amfterdam, 1703, *fo. & à la Haye,* 1730, *fo.*

EGMONT VAN DER NYENBURG (J. AEGID VAN) en Hoymann (Jo.) reifen door een gedeelte van Europa, Klein Afia, Archipel, &c. Leiden, 1757 & 1758, 4to. 2 deele.

KLEEMANN's (NIC. ERNST) Reife von Wienn über Belgrad bis Kilianova, &c. Wienn 1771, 8vo. Leipzig, 1773, 8vo. Prag. 1783, 8vo.

Ditto, in French, 1780, *8vo. A Hamburg,* 1780, *8vo.*

MATHEWS (DOCTOR) voyage en France, en Italie, & aux ifles de l'Archipel en 1750, traduit de l'Anglois, par Monf. de Puiffeux. A Paris, 1763, gr. 12mo. 4 tom.

PALERNE (JEAN) peregrinations en Egypte, Arabie, Terre Sainte, Syrie, Natolie, Grece, & les ifles. A Lyon, 1606, 12mo.

PASCH DI KRIENEN (CONTA LION) breve defcrizione dell' Arcipelago. In Livorno, 1773, 8vo.

PIACENZA (FRANC.) Egeo redivivo, o fia chorografia dell' Arcipelago. In Modena, 1688.

Po-

Pocock's (Rich.) Description of the East. London, 1743, 1745, fo. 2 vol.
Ditto, in German. Erlangen, 1754, 1755, 4to. 3 Th. überfetzt von Windheim.
Ditto. Erlangen, 1771, 1773, 4to. 3 Th. uberfetzt von Schreber.
Ditto, in French. A Paris, & Neufchatel, 1772, 12mo. 6 tom.
Ditto, in Dutch; t' Utrecht, 1780, gr. 4to.
Sommer's (Jan.) zee-en land-reife naer de Levant, namelyk Italien, Candien, Cyprus, Egypten, Rhodus, Archipel, Turkien, en door Duitfchland. t'Amfterdam, 1649—1661, 4to.
Thevenot (Nich. Melch de) voyage au Levant, contenant diverfes particularités de l'Archipel. A Paris, 1665, 4to.
Tournefort (Jean Pillon de) relation d'un voyage du Levant, contenant l'hiftoire ancienne & moderne de plufieurs ifles de l'Archipel, &c. A Paris, 1712, 4to. II tom. A Lyon, 1717. gr. 8vo. III tom. A Amfterdam, 1728, gr. 4to. II tom.
Ditto in German. Nurnberg, 1776, 1777, gr. 8vo. III Bande.
Welschen's (Hieron) Reifebefchreibung nach Italien, die Infeln des Mittellandifchen Meers, &c. Stutgard, 1658, 4to. Nurnberg, 1658, 4to. Stutgard, 1664, 4to.

ASSOW

ASSOW. (THE SEA OF)

SCYLACIS (CARYANDENSIS) Periplus maris Mediterranei. Anonymi periplus Moeotidis palus, & Ponti Euxini;
Agathemeri hypothypofis geographiae: Omnia Graeco-Latina; Anonymi expeditio totius mundi Latina: Cum notis (Js.) Voffii (Jac.) Palmerii (S.) Jchullii; ex emendatione (Jac.) Gronovii. Lugd. 1700. 4to.

ASTURIAS.

CASAL (GASP) Hiftoria natural y medica del principado de Afturias. Madrid, 1762, 4to.

ATHENS.

HACKLUYT'S (RICH.) vide ANGLESEY.

ATHOS. (MOUNT)

GEORGIERENES (JOSEPH) Befchreibung des gegenwärtigen Zuftandes der Infeln Samos

Samos, Nicaria, Pathmos, wie auch des Berges Athos; aus dem Griechifchen uberfetzt. 1689, 12mo.

AUVERGNE.

GIRAUD SOULAVIE (ABBE) hiftoire naturelle de la France Meridionale, ou recherche fur la mineralogie du Vivarais, du Viennois, du Forez, de l'Auvergne, du Velai, &c. fur la phyfique de la mer Mediterranée, fur les meteores, les arbres, les animaux, l'homme; & la femme de ces contrées. Nifmes, 1780, 1781. gr. 8vo. III tom.

AUNIS.

ARCERE (D') Hiftoire naturelle du païs d' Aunis, de fes côtes, & des provinces limitrophes. A Paris, 1757, 4to.

AUSTRIA.

BERNOUILLI's (JOH.) Sammlung kleiner Reifebefchreibungen. Leipzig, 1781, 1783, 8vo. XII Bändchen.

BROWN's (EDW.) Account of fome travels in different parts of Europe, viz. Hungary Servia,

Servia, Bulgaria, Macedonia, Theffaly, Auftria, Stiria, Carinthia, Carniola, Friule, Germany, Low Countries, Lombardy, &c. with obfervations on the gold, filver, &c. mines, baths, and mineral waters, and defcriptions of antiquities, &c. London, 1673, 4to. London, 1685, fol.

Ditto in French. A Paris, 1674, 4to. 1684, 4to.
Ditto in Dutch. Amfterdam, 1682, 4to.
Ditto in German. Nurnberg, 1686, & 1711, 4to.

CASINI DE THURY Relation de deux voyages en Allemagne par ordre du Roi, pour determiner la grandeur du degré de longitude. A Paris, 1763, 4to.

------- Relation d'un voyage en Allemagne, qui comprend les operations relatives à la figure de la terre, & à la geographie particuliere du Palatinat, d'Autriche, &c. A Paris, 1776, 4to.

EDELINGII (JOACH.) hodoeporicon Bohemicum, Auftriacum, Hungaricum. Roftock, 1571, 8vo.

HERMANN's (BEN. FRANZ.) Reifen durch Oefterreich, Steyermark, Carnthen, &c. im Jahr, 1780, Wienn, 1781, 1782. 1783, 8vo. III Theile.

-------- Abrifs der phyficalifchen Befchaffenheit der Oefterreichifchen Staten, und des gegenwärtigen Zuftandes der Landwirthfchaft, Gewerbe, Manufacturen, Fabriken

quelle im Stift Bafil. Genf, 1756, 8vo.
Itineraire alphabetique de la ville de Bâle,
de fes environs, &c. à l'ufage des voyageurs. A Bâle, 1782, 12mo.

BAVARIA.

BERNOULLI (JOH.) vide AUSTRIA.
BIANCONI (GIO. LOD.) Lettere al Marchefe
Ercolani fopra alcune particolaritá della
Baviera, ed altri paefi della Germania
In Lucca, 1763, 8vo.
-------- Merkwürdigkeiten des Churbayerifchen Hofes. Leipzig, 1764, 8vo.
CASINI DE THURY, vide AUSTRIA.
EINZINGER'S VON EINZING (J. MART. MAR.)
phyficalifcher Abrifs des heutigen Churfurftenthums Bayern. Munchen, 1767, 8vo.
2 Th.
---------- Politifcher Abrifs von Bayern.
Munchen, 1777, 8vo. 2 Theile.
GERKEN'S (PHIL. WILH.) Reife durch Schwaben, Bayern, &c. in den Jahren, 1779,
1783, nebft Nachrichten von Bibliotheken,
Handfchriften, Römifchen Alterthümern,
politifchen Verfaffungen, Landwirthfchaft
und Landes-produften, &c. Stendal, 1786,
gr. 8vo. III Theile.
Gefammelte Anzeige zur phyfifchen und politifchen

tifchen kenntnifs von Bayern, der Oberpfalz, Neuburg, und Salzbach. Frankf. 1786 8vo.

HERMAN (B. FR.) *vide* AUSTRIA.

LOMENII ITINERARIUM *vide* AUSTRIA.

PEZZL'S (JOH.) Reife durch den Bayerifchen Kreifs. Saltzburg & Leipzig, 1784, 8vo.

REMARQUES HISTORIQUES, *vide* AUSTRIA.

SULZER (FRANZ. JOS.) *vide* AUSTRIA.

Tagebuch eines Hofmeifters auf einer Reife durch den Fränkifchen Kreis nach Carlsbad und durch Bayern. Erlangen, 1787, 8vo. 1ter. Theil.

WEKHERLIN (FRANZ. JOS.) *vide* AUSTRIA.

ZAPF (G. W.) Litterarifche Reifen. Augfburg, 1782, 1783, gr. 8vo.

BEAUJOLOIS.

BRISSON, Memoire hiftorique & oeconomique fur le Beaujolois. A Avignon, 1770, 8vo.

DULAC (ALLEON) hiftoire naturelle des provinces du Lionnois, Forez, & Beaujolois. A Lyon, 1765, 8vo. II tom.

BED-

BEDFORDSHIRE.

Sketch of a tour into Derbyshire and Yorkshire, including part of Buckingham—Warwick—Leicester—Nottingham—Northampton—Bedford—and Hartfordshire. London, 1778. Ditto 1785, 8vo.

BELGRAD.

KLEEMANN (NIC. ERNST) *vide* ARCHIPELAGO.

BELLENTZ.

SCHINZ (HANS RUDOLF) Beyträge zur nähern kenntnifs des Schweitzerlandes. Zuich, 1784, 1785, 8vo. 2ter. & 3ter. Heft.

BELLUNO.

BERNOULLI'S (JOH.) Archiv zur neuen Geschichte; Geographie, Natur—und Menschen—Kenntnifs. Leipzig, 1785, 1786, gr. 8vo, V Theile.

BERGAMO.

MALTONI (G.) fulla ftoria naturale della provincia Bergamafca. In Bergamo, 1782, 8vo.

BERLIN.

Ausführliche Befchreibung der Reife S. K. Hoheit des G. F. von Rufsland, Paul Petrowitz von Peterfburg nach Berlin, und zuruck. Berlin, 1776, gr. 8vo.

BERNOULLI'S (JOH.) *vide* BELLUNO.

Neue Reifebemerkungen in und über Deutfchland von verfchiedenen Verfaffern. Halle, 1786, 8vo. 2 Bände. Hall, 1787, 3ter Band.

O (C. H.) Bemerkungen auf einer Reife von Berlin nach Bromberg in Weft Preuffen. Berlin & Leipzig, 1784, 8vo.

Reife im Sommer 1780 nach Pyrmont, Braunfchweig, Berlin, &c. Hannover, 1784, 8vo.

Reife von Wienn uber Prag, Drefden, Laufnitz nach Berlin. Leipzig, 1787, 8vo.

SHERLOCK (MART.) Lettres d'un voyageur Anglois en divers endroits de l'Europe. Geneve, 1779. 12mo.

The fame in Englifh. London 1779, 1781, *8vo.*
The fame in German. Frankfurt & Leipzig, 1780, *8vo.*

— neue

------ neue Briefe auf feiner Reife nach Italien, Genf, Laufanne, Strafburg, Berlin, &c. Leipzig, 1782, 8vo. Aus dem Französifchen.

TOLLII (JAC.) epiftolae itinerariae; iter Beroli̇nenfe, &c. *Amfterdam* 1700, 4to. *Amfterdam*, 1714, 4to.

TROSCHELS (JAC. ELIAS) Reife von Berlin nach den Schlefifchen Gebirge im Sommer 1783. Berlin, 1784, 8vo.

BLACK SEA.

ARRIANI (FLAVI) Pontis Euxini & Maris Erythraei periplus Graece, cum Latina verfione & fcholiis, additis praeter loca, quae folers penetravit Lufitanorum navigatio, oppidis, quae Danubius irrigat. Auctore Stuckio. Geneve 1577, folio.

CHARDIN (JEAN) Journal du voyage en Perfe, &c. A Amfterdam 1735, 4to. IV tom.

SCYLACIS periplus Maris Mediterranei, *vide* Assow.

TOURNEFORT, relation d'un voyage au Levant. *Vide* ARCHIPELAGO.

BLANC. (MOUNT)

BOURRIT (M. Th.) *vide* ALPS.

BLANCK-

BLANCKENBURGH.

BERNOULLI (JOH.) *vide* AUSTRIA.
Neue Reifebemerkungen in und uber Deutfchland, *vide* BERLIN.

BLOCKSBERG.

RITTERI (ALBERTI) Relatio hiftorica curiofa de iterato itinere in Hercyniae montem famofiffimum Brufterum. Helmft. 1740, 4to.

BOHEMIA.

BENJAMINIS NAVARRENI itinerarium, *vide* EUROPE.
BERNOULLI (JOH.) *vide* AUSTRIA.
BURNEY'S (CARL) Tagebuch feiner muficalifchen Reifen, aus dem Englifchen. Hamburg, 1772, 1773, 8vo. III Th.
EDELINGII (JOACH.) hodoeporicon, *vide* AUSTRIA.
FERBER's (J.) Beytrage zu der mineral Gefchichte von Böhmen. Berlin, 1774, gr. 8vo.

FERBER's (J.) neue Beyträge zur mineral Geschichte verschiedener Länder. Mietau,
1778, gr. 8vo.
HEBERER VON BRETTEN, vide DENMARK.
KEYSLER's (JOHN GEORGE) travels through
Germany, Bohemia, Hungary, Switzerland, Italy, &c. London, 1760.
The same translated into German. Hannover, 1740,
1751, 1776, 4to. II Th.
MAYER Le Comte de Falkenstein, ou voyages
de l'Empereur Joseph II. en Italie en Boheme, & en France. A Rome, & A Paris,
1777, 12mo.
The same in German. Leipzig, 1777, 8vo.
PARIZEK's (ALEXIUS) kurtzgefaste Naturgeschichte Böhmens. Prag, 1784, 4to.
PATIN (CHARLES) Relations historiques &
curieuses des voyages en Allemagne, Boheme, Angleterre, &c. Strasbourg, 1670,
12mo. Bâle, 1673, 12mo. Lyon, 1674,
12mo. Rouen, 1676, 12mo. Amsterdam,
1695, gr. 12mo.
The same in Italian, translated by Bulifon. Venezia,
1685, 12mo.
POCOCK's (RICH.) vide ARCHIPELAGO.
Remarques historiques, vide AUSTRIA,
Remarques historiques & critiques, vide AUS-
TRIA.
SCHALLER's (GAROSL) Topographie von Böhmen. Prag & Wien, 1787, 8vo.

BOS-

BOSPHORUS OF THRACE.

GYLLII (PETRI) tractatus de Bofphoro Thracico libri III. Lugduni, 1561, 4to. Lugd. 1632, 24mo.

MARSIGLI (LUIGI FERD. CONTE) offervazioni intorno al Bofphoro Thracico, overo Canale di Conftantinopoli. In Roma, 1681, 4to.

BOTHNIA.

RUDBECK'S (OLOF) *vide* ALAND.
SCHELLER'S (JOH. GERK.) Reifebefchreibung von Lappland und Bothnien. Jena, 1713, 1727, 1748, 8vo.

BRABANT.

CALVETE DE ESTRELLA (JUAN CHRISTOVAL) Viage del Principe Don Felipe, hijo del Emperador Carlos V. desde Efpaña a fus tierras de la Baxa Alemannia, con la defcripcion de todos los eftados del Brabante y Flandes. En Anverfa, 1552, fo.

CAN-

CANTILLON (DE) Delices de Brabant, & de les campagnes. A Amsterdam, 1758, 8vo. II tom.

DESCHAMPS (J. B.) voyage pittoresque de la Flandres & du Brabant. A Paris, 1769, 8vo.

The same in German. Leipzig, 1771, 8vo.

ORTELII (ABRAH.) itinerarium Gallo-Brabanticum. Lugd. 1630, 24mo. Lugd. 1647, 12mo.

PAYEN Voyages avec une description de l'Angleterre, de la Flandre, & du Brabant. A Paris, 1663 & 1668, 12mo.

The same in Italian, translated by LAURENTI. *In* Torino, 1685, 12mo.

SAINT MARTIN (MICHAEL DE) Relation d'un voyage fait en Flandre, Brabant, &c. A Caen, 1667, 12mo.

The tour of Holland through Brabant, &c. London, 1772, 12mo.

BRANDENBURGH.

APELBLAD (JON.) Resebeskrifning öfwer Pommern, och Brandenburg. Stockholm, 1757, 8vo.

BERNOULLI (JOH.) *vide* AUSTRIA & COURLAND.

BEN-

BENECKENDORF (CARL FRID. VON) kleine oeconomifche Reifen in die Neu und Mittelmark. Zullichau, gr. 8vo. 2 Th.

BRAND JOH. (ARNOLD VON) Reifen durch Brandenburg, Preuffen, &c. Wefel, 1702, 8vo.

- - - - - *in Dutch.* Utrecht, 1703, 8vo.

BUCHWALD (FR. VON) occonomifche und ftatiftifche Reife durch Mecklenburg, Pommern, Holftein, und Brandenburg; aus Dem Danifchen. Copenhagen, 1786, gr. 8vo.

BURNEY (CARL) *vide* BOHEMIA.

DENINA'S (ABT.) Brandenburgifche Briefe, aus dem Italienifchen uberfetzt. Berlin, 1786, 8vo.

BREMEN.

Reife im Sommer, 1780, *vide* BERLIN.

Vermifchte Abhandlungen zur Erläuterung der Naturgefchichte des Hertzogthums Bremen und Verden. Bremen, 1759, 8vo.

ZEILLER's (M.) defcriptio regnorum Sweciae Gothiae, Finlandiae, Livoniae, Bremenfis ducatus, Pommeraniae, &c. Amfterdam, 1665, 12mo.

BRESCIA.

PILATI (CHRISTOPHORO) Saggio di ſtoria naturale del Breſciano. In Breſcia, 1769, 4to.

BRUNSWICK.

Reiſe im Sommer, 1780, *vide* BERLIN.

BRUSSELS.

Voyage de Spa à Bruxelles. A Bruxelles, 1783, 8vo.

BUCKINGHAM.

Sketch of a tour into Derbyſhire, &c. *vide* BEDFORDSHIRE.

BULGARIA.

BOSCOWICH (RUGHIERO GIUS.) giornale di un viaggio da Conſtantinopoli, &c. in Polonia. In Boſſano, 1784, 8vo.

CADIX.

HACKLUYT (RICH.) *vide* ANGLESEY.
Neue Sammlung von Reifebefchreibungen, &c. Hamburg, gr. 8vo. 6ter Band von PLA-
TIERE.
VOLCKARD'S (ADR. GOTTL.) *vide* AMSTER-
DAM.

CANARY ISLANDS.

Allgemeine Hiftorie der Reifen zu Waffer und zu Lande. Leipzig, 1747, 4to. XXI Bände.

BENZONI (GIROL.) iftoria del mondo nuovo, libri III. In Venezia, 1565, 8vo. con la giunta di alcune cofe notabili delle ifole di Canarìa. In Venezia, 1572, 8vo.

The fame in Dutch. Haerlem, 1610, 8vo.

The fame in Latin. Genevae, 1578, 1581, 1600, 8vo.

The fame in German. Bafil. 1579, 1582, fo. Hamburg, 1648, 4to.

BONTHIER & VERRIER, hiftoire de la premiere decouverte, & de la conquête des Canaries, 1402. A Paris, 1630, 8vo.

DAPPER (O) Befchryving der Africaenfche eylanden,

eylanden, als Madagafcar, St. Thome, Kanarien, Kaep de Verd, Malta. Amfterdam, 1668. fol.

– – – – – Befchreibung von Afrika. Amfterd. 1670. fol.

– – – – – Defcription de l'Afrique. Amfterdam, 1686, fo.

GLASS's (GEORG) Gefchichte der Entdeckung und Eroberung der Canarifchen Infuln größtentheiles von einer in der Infel, Palma gefundenen Handfchrift von Juan d' Abreu di Galineo. Leipzig, 1777, 8vo. Nebft einer eigenen Befchreibung diefer Infeln.

– – – – – Hiftory of the difcovery and conqueft of the Canary Iflands. London, 1764, 4to.

KUEHN's (JOH. MICH.) Lebens und Reifebefchreibung nach Groenland, Spitzbergen, Straffe David's, Canarifchen Infeln, Liffabon, Algier, &c. Gotha, 1741, 8vo. Do. Nordhaufen, 1784, 8vo. Mit einem Plan von Algier.

MAIRE (LE) Voyages aux Illes Canaries, Cap Verd, &c. 1695, 12mo.

NUN'EZ DE PEN'A (JUAN) Conquifta, y antiguedades de la illa de la Gran Canaria, y fu defcripcion. Madrid, 1676.

ROBERT's (GEORGE) voyage to the Canary iflands, &c. London, 1726, 8vo.

VI-

VIERA Y CLAOJO (JOS. DE) Noticias de la hiftoria general de las iflas de Canarias. En Madrid, 1771. 8vo. III vol.

CANDIA.

A defcription of Candia, 1670, 12mo.
DAPPER, vide ARCHIPELAGO.
PIACENZA, vide Do.
POCOCKE, vide Do.
SAVINION D'ALQUIE (FR.) Hiftoire curieufe du Siege de Candie, 1670, & 1671, II tom.
SOMMERS (JAN.) vide ARCHIPELAGO.
TOTT (BARON DE) Memoires fur les Turcs & fur les Tartares. Amfterdam, 1784, gr. 8vo. IV parties.

CARINTHIA.

BROWN (EDWARD) vide AUSTRIA.
GRISELINI (FRANC.) Lettere odoporiche di Venezia, Triefte, Carinthia, &c. colle offervazioni fpettanti alla ftoria naturale. In Milano, 1780, 4to.
HERMANN (B. FR.) vide AUSTRIA.
REMARQUES HISTORIQUES, vide Do.

CARNIOLA.

BROWN (EDW.) *vide* AUSTRIA.

CHURELICHZ (LAURENT DE) Narratio itineris in Styriam Carinthiam, & Carniolam, Leopoldi 1mi. Viennae, 1661, 8vo.

GRASSI DI FORMEASO (NICOL.) Notizie storiche della provincia della Carnia. In Udina, 1782 8vo.

GRISELINI, *vide* CARINTHIA.

GRUBER (JOH.) Briefe hydrographifchen und phyficalifchen Inhalts aus Krain. Wienn, 1781, gr. 8vo.

HACQUET Orytographia Carniolica. Leipzig, 1776, 1783. gr. 4to. III Th.

HACQUET (B.) *vide* ALPS.

─ ─ ─ ─ ─ ─ Mineralogifche botanifche Reife von dem Berg Terglou in Krain zu den Berg Glockner in Tyrol, 1779, 1781. Wienn, 1784, 8vo

HERMANN (B. F.) *vide* AUSTRIA.

Remarques hiftoriques *vide* AUSTRIA.

Remarques hiftoriques & critiques, *vide* Do.

CASSEL.

Briefe eines Reifenden über den gegenwärtigen

Zuf-

Zuftand von Caffel. Frankfurt & Leipzig, 1781.
Briefe eines Reifenden von Pyrmont, &c. nach Caffel, Marburg, Wurtzburg und Wilhelmsbad. Franf. 1783, 8vo.
Neue Reifebemerkungen in und uber Deutschland, *vide* BERLIN.

CATALONIA:

THICKNESSE (PHIL.) A year's journey through France and a part of Spain. London, 1777, 8vo. II vol.

CEFALONIA.

DAPPER (OLIVER) Befchryving van Morea en de eylanden van de Adriadtfche zee, Korfu, Cefalonia, Santa Maura, & Zanten. Amfterdam. 1683, fol.
MOROSINI (AND.) Corfi di penna fopra l'ifola di Cefalonia, in Venezia, 1628. 4to.

CHAMPAIGN.

R (COMTE GREGOIRE DE) voyage mineralogique et phyfique de Bruxelles à Laufanne par une partie de Luxembourg, de la Lorraine, Champagne, et Franche Comté fait en 1782. A Lauſanne, et à Bern, 1783, 8vo.

CHANTILLY.

A tour to Ermenonville, containing beſides an account of the palace, gardens, and curioſities of Chantilly, and of the Marquis de Girardin's beautiful ſeat of Ermenonville, a particular deſcription of the tomb of J. J. Rouſſeau, with anecdotes never before publiſhed. London, 1785, 8vo.

CHERSO in the ADRIATIC.

FORTIS (ALB.) Saggio d'oſſervazioni ſopra l'iſola di Cherſo ed Oſero. In Venezia, 1777, 4to.

CHESHIRE.

LEIGH's (CHARLES) Natural Hiſtory of Lancaſhire, Cheſhire, and the peak of Derbyſhire. Oxford, 1700. folio.

The hiſtory of Cheſhire, containing King's Vale Royal entire, &c. Cheſter, 8vo. II. vols.

CLOUD (SAINT)

SAUGRAIN (CLAUDE) Curiosités de Paris, de Versailles, de Marly, de Vincennes, de St. Cloud, &c. A Paris 1716, 12mo.
Voyage de Paris à St Cloud. A Paris. 1754, 12mo.

COLOGNE.

Kleine Reisen. Lecture für dillettanten. Berlin, 1785, 1786. 8vo. III Bände.

COMPOSTELLA.

HEIDEGGERI (JO. HENR.) dissertatio de peregrinationibus religiosis, in specie Hierosolimitana, Romana, Compostellensi, Lauretana, et Eremitana Helvetiorum. Tigur. 1670. 8vo.

CONSTANCE.

HUINLIN's (DAVID) Beschreibung des Boden-See nach seinen verschiedenen Zustand in altern ältern und neuern Zeiten, Ulm, und Lindau, 1783, gr. 8vo.

SANDER's Reife nach Coftnitz und Schaffhaufen, im 3ten Band in BERNOULLI's SAMMLUNG, *vide* AUSTRIA.

CONSTANTINOPLE.

ALMOSNINO (R. MOYSES) Eftremos y grandezas de Conftantinopla. En Madrid, 1638, 4to.

ARVIEUX (LAURENT DE) Memoires contenant les voyages à Conftantinople, &c. Paris, 1735, gr. 12mo. VI tom.

BALTIMORE's (FR. LORD) Tour to the Eaft in 1763 and 1764, with remarks on the city of Conftantinople. London, 1767. 8vo.

The fame in German. Leipzig, 1768, gr. 8vo.

BALAM (CLAS) Conftantinopolitanifche Refa. Stockh. 1679, 4to.

BELL's (JOHN) Travels from St Peterfburg in Ruffia to different parts of Afia. Glafgow, 1763, 4to. II vol.

The fame in French. A Paris, 1766, 12mo. *III vol.*

BENAGLIA (GIOR.) Relazione del viaggio fatto dal Conte Alberto Caprara. In Roma, 1684, 12mo.

The fame in German. Frankfurt, 1687, 8vo.

BENEVENGA (MICH.) Viaggio di Levante, colla defcrizione di Conftantinopoli. In Bologna, 1688, 12mo.

Befchreibung einer Reife eines Pohlnifchen Bothfchafters gen Conftantinopel und in die Tartarey. Nurnberg, 1571, 4to.

BESOLT'S VON LICHTENSTEIN (MELCHIOR) Reifen nach Conftantinopel, 1584, fol.

BJOERNSTAHEL (JAC. JAN) Refa till Frankrycke, Italien, Sweitz, Tyfkland, Holland, Aengland, Turkiet, och Grekeland. Stockholm, 1777, 1780, 8vo. V Delar.

BJOERNSTAEHL's Briefe auf feinen aufländifchen Reifen durch Frankreich, Italien, Schweitz, Deutfchland, Holland, England, Turkey, Griechenland, &c. Leipzig und Roftock, 1777. 1782, 1783, 8vo. VI Bände.

CASTEL (J. DE) Voiages de François Savary en Grece, Terre Sainte, Conftantinople, &c. jufqu'en 1605. A Paris, 1628, & 1630, 4to.

COLLIER (JUSTIN) Refident à la porte pour les Etats Generaux Unies en 1668, journal du voyage. A Paris, 1672, 12mo.

DAES (JOVIS VON DER) verfcheide voyagien gedaan na Conftantinopolen, &c. 1652, 12mo.

DOUSAC (GEORG.) De itinere fuo Conftantinopolitano epiftolae; accedunt veteres

fcriptiones ex Byzantio & reliqua Graeciæ
Lugd. 1599, 8vo.

DRIESCHII (GBRH. CON.) hiftoria magnae legationis Caefareae, quam Caroli VI. auſpiciis fufcepit Comes Damianus Hugo Virmontius ad Portam Ottomannicam. Viennae, 1721, 8vo.

F. (J. F.) Die Donau Reife, das ift kurtzgefafte Nachricht von den Stroemen, &c. welche der Donau zugebracht werden nebft angrenzenden Provintzen: Ingleichen eine Marfch-Route von Belgrad bis Conftantinopel Regenfburg, 1760, 8vo.

FURER's (CHRISTOPH.) Conftantinopolitanifche Reife. Nurnberg, 1646, 4to.

GASSOT (JAC.) Relation du voyage de Venife, à Conftantinople. A Bourges, 1684, 12mo.

GERLACH's (STEPHAN) Tagebuch der von Maximilian IIten. und Rudolph II. an die Ottomannifche Pforte abgefertigten und durch David Ungnad Freyherrn von Sonnegh vollbrachten Gefandfchaft. Frankfurt, 1674, fol.

GRELOT (Jos.) Relation nouvelle d'un voyage de Conftantinople. A Paris, 1680, 4to. 1681, 1vo.

HACKLUYT (RICH.) vide ANGLESEY.

KLEEMANN (NIC. ERNST.) vide ARCHIPELAGO.

KUS-

KUSZEWICZ (SAM.) Narratio legationis Zharavianae & rerum apud Othomannos, 1622, geſtarum. Dantiſci, 1645, 4to. 1653, 4to.

L. (P. M.) Voyage de Mr. Quielet à Conſtantinople par terre. A Paris, 1660, 8vo. 1664, 12mo.

LISLE's Brief von Conſtantinopel, 1786: zu finden in den Kleinen Reiſen, *vide* COLOGNE.

MAGNI (COM.) Quanto di piu curioſo e vago ha potuto raccorre nel primo biennio, 1672. 1673 da lui conſumato in viaggi per la Turchia, &c. Parma, 1679, 12mo. Venezia, 1682, 12mo. Bologna, 1615, 12mo.

MONCONYS (BARTH. DE) Journal des voyages en Europe, Aſie, Afrique, &c. A Lyon, 1665, & 1666, 4to. 3 vol. A Paris, 1667, 4to. III vol. A Paris, 1695, gr. 12mo. V tom.

MUNTZER VON BABENBERG (WOLFGANG) Reiſebeſchreibung von Venedig aus nach Jeruſalem, Damaſcus, & Conſtantinopel im Jahr 1556. Nurnberg, 1624, 4to.

NORBERG's Brief aus Italien & Conſtantinopel. Leipzig & Roſtock, 1783, 8vo.

PERRY's (CHARLES) View of the Levant, particularly of Conſtantinople, Syria, Egypt, and Greece, London, 1743, fol.

PÒRSII (HENR.) Itineris Byzantini defcriptio. Fraucof. 1583, 8vo.

POSER (HEINR. VON.) Tagebuch feiner Reife von Conftantinopel durch Bulgarien, Armenien, Perfien, und Indien. Jena, 1675, 4to.

Raccolta di varii viaggi fatti da Venezia alla Tartaria, &c. In Venezia, 1543, 8vo.

RANZOW (JOH. VON) Reifebefchreibung nach Jerufalem, Cairo, & Conftantinopel. Copenhagen, 1669, 4to. Hamburg, 1704, 8vo.

Reife und Bothfchaft des Reichfgrafen von Leflie an die Ottomannifche Pforte. Breflau, 1680, 12mo.

SCHWEIGGER'S (SALOMON) Reifebefchreibung aus Deutfchland nach Conftantinopel & Jerufalem. Nurnberg, 1608, 4to. Do. 1614, 1619, 1639, 1664.

SAPIENZA (OTTAV.) Nuevo tratado de Turquia, con una defcripcion de Conftantinopla. En Madrid, 1622, 4to.

SEIDEL's FRID.) Denckwürdige Gefandfchaft an die Ottommannifche Pforte auf Kayfer Rudolph des IIten. Befehl von Frid. von Kreckwitz verrichtet, nebft Anmerkungen heraus gegeben von Haufdorf. Görlitz, 1711, 8vo. unter den Titel: Merckwürdige Reifebefchreibung aus Deutfch-

Deutschland, über Wien, Oesterreich, & Hungarn bis Constantinopel. Leipzig, 1773, 8vo.

SESTINI (DOM.) Lettere odoporiche. In Livorno, 1784, 1785, 8vo. II vol.

▲------ Beschreibung des Canals von Constantinopel, des dasigen Wein—Acker —und Garten— Baues, und der Jagd der Türken. Aus dem Ital. Hamburg, 1786, 8vo.

SIMPERTI Diarium, oder, Reisebeschreibung Wolfgangs Grafen von Oettingen K. Grosbothschafter nach Constantinopel von 1691, bis 1701. Augsburg, 1701, 8vo.

STAMMER (ARND GEBH. VON) Morgenländische Reisebeschreibung nach Constantinopel, Egypten, & Jerusalem. Gera, 1670, 12mo. Jena, 1675, 12mo.

THEVENOT (NIC. MELCH. DE) vide ARCHIPELAGO.

TOLLOT, Voyage fait au Levant aux années, 1731 & 1732, contenant les descriptions d'Alger, Tunis, Tripoli, Alexandrie, Terre Sainte, Constantinople, &c. A Paris, 1742, 12mo.

TOTT (BARON DE) Memoires sur les Turcs & sur les Tartares. Amsterdam, 1784, 8vo. IV parties. A Paris, 1785, gr. 12mo. en II tom.

Ditto in English. London, 1785, 8vo.

Ditto

Ditto in German. Elbingen, 1785, 8vo. 3 Th.

TOURNEFORT, *vide* ARCHIPELAGO.

TROIL'S (FRANZ FERD. VON) Orientalifche Reifebefchreibung- Drefden, 1764, 4to. Leipzig, 1717, 8vo. Drefden & Leipzig, 1734, 8vo.

WENNER's (ADAM) Befchreibung der Legation und Reife, abgeordnet von Mathias 2ten. an den Turkifchen, Kayfer, Achmet 1ten. von 1616, bis 1618, Nurnberg, 1622 & 1665, 4to.

WILDEN's (JOH.) Reifebefchreibung eines gefangenen Chriften. Nurnberg, 1613, 4to. Do. 1623.

WRATISLAW (FRH. VON.) Merkwürdige Gefandfchaft's Reife von Wienn nach Conftantinopel. Leipzig, 1786, 8vo.

COPENHAGEN.

BUNAU (GRAF) Reife von Hamburg nach Copenhagen; in Bernoulli's Sammlung's 8ten. Band; *vide* AUSTRIA.

WILSE (J. N.) Reife von Chriftiania nach Copenhagen, 1764; in Bernoulli's Sammlung 13ten Band; *vide* AUSTRIA.

WRAXALL's (NATHAN) Curfory remarks made in a tour through fome of the Northern parts

parts of Europe, particularly Copenhagen, Stockholm and Peterfburg. London, 1775, 8vo.

C O R F U.

DAPPER, *vide* ARCHIPELAGO.
MARMORA (AND.) della ftoria di Corfu. In Venezia. 1672, 4to.

C O R K.

SMITH's (CH.) Ancient and prefent ftate of the county of Cork. Dublin. 1750, 8vo.

C O R N W A L L.

BORLASE's (WILL.) Natural hiftory of Cornwall, &c. Oxford. 1758. fol. London, 1759, fol.
CAREW's (RICH.) Survey of Cornwall. London, 1602, 4to. do. 1723, 4to.

C O R S I C A.

BARRAL Memoire fur l' hiftoire naturelle de Corfe

Corfe. A Londres; & se trouve, à Paris 1783. 12mo.

BELLIN Description geographique & historique de l' isle de Corse. 'A Paris. 1769, 4to avec 32 cartes.

BOSWELL'S (JAMES) Account of Corsica, with the journal of a tour to that island, and memoirs of Pascal P. di. ' Glasgow, 1768, gr. 8vo. III edition with some additions. London, 1769, gr. 8vo.

The same in French. A la Haye, 1769.

BOSWELL, Etat de Corse *translated from the English.* 'A Paris, 1769, 8vo.

The same in German, translated by A. E. Klaus-sing. Leipzig, 1768, 8vo. do. 1769.

The same in Italian, translated from the original. Londra, 1769, 4to. con 1 carta geografica.

B. (F. X.) Briefe über die von der Cron Frankreich gemachte Eroberung von Corsica, denen in F. Boswell's Beschreibung aufgestellten Gründen entgegen gesetzt, &c. Frankfurt & Leipz. 1770.

Description de la Corse, avec la relation de la derniere guerre. A Paris, 1743, 12mo.

GRISALVI (STRATANEO) storia naturale dell' isola di Corsica. In Firenze. 1774, 8vo.

HASENOEHRL Storia naturale dell' isola di Corsica. In Firenze, 1774, 8vo.

JAUSSIN, Memoires historiques sur l' histoire naturelle

naturelle de l'iſle de Corſe. A Lauſanne, 1758.

LAMBERG (MAXIMILIAN GRAF VON) Tagebuch eines Weltmans über Italien, und Corſica; überſetzt aus dem Franzöſiſchen von H. L. Wagner. Frankfurt, 1775, 8vo.

MERTEN'S (HIER. AND.) Beſchreibung von Corſica. Augſburg, 1769, 8vo.

Oſſervazioni d'un viaggiatore Ingleſe ſopra l' iſola di Corſica. In Londra, 1768, 8vo.

PUY (FERRAND DE) Eſſai chronologique, hiſtorique. & politique de Corſe. 'A Paris, 1777, 12mo.

SCHLÖZER'S (AUG. LUD,) Kleine Weltgeſchichte No. 1. Corſica. Göttingen & Gotha, 1770, 16mo.

SINGLADE Mémoires & voyages en Corſe, Naples, Rome, Allemagne, Flandres, & France. 'A Paris, 1765, 8vo. II tom.

VOGT'S (JOH.) Beſchreibung der Inſel Corſica. Nurnberg & Altdorf, 1735, 4to.

COURLAND.

BERNOUILLI's (JOH.) Reiſen durch Brandenburg, Pommern, Preuſſen, Curland, Ruſſland, und Pohlen. Leipzig, 1779, 1780, 8vo. VI Bände.

The same in French. A Varsovie, 1782, 8vo.

BRAND (JOH. ARN. VON.) *vide* BRANDENBURG.

BURJA (ABEL) Obfervations d' un voyageur fur la Ruffie, la Finlande, la Livonie, la Courlande, et la Pruffe; avec un fupplement a l' êtat de la Ruffie de Mr. Wenzel. A Berlin, 1785, 8vo.

FISCHER'S (JACOB. BENJ.) Zufätze zu feinem Verfuch der Naturgefchichte von Liefland nebft FERBERS (JOH. JAC.) Anmerkungen zur phyfifchen Erdbefchreibung von Curland. Riga, 1784. 8vo.

MAYER'S Briefe eines jungen Reifenden durch Liefland, Curland, und Deutfchland. Erlangen, 1777, 8vo. II Theile.

C R I M.

BEAUPLAN (GUIL. LE VASSEUR DE) Defcription de l' Ukraine &c. A Rouen, 1640, 4to. do. 1660. 4to.

-------- Befchreibung der Ukraine, der Krim, und deren Einwohnern, überfetzt mit Anmerkungen, und einem Anhang aus dem Tagebuch von Printz Maximilian von Wurtemberg, der die Ukraine betrift, von Ioh. Wilh. Moeller. Breflau, 1780, 8vo.

KLEEMANN, (N. E.) *vide* ARCHIPELAGO.

Kleine

Kleine Reifen, *vide* COLOGNE.

MOTRAYE (AUBRY DE LA) Travels through Europe, Afia, &c, containing a great variety of geographical, topographical and political obfervations, efpecially on Italy, Turkey, Greece, Crim, Noghai-Tartary, Circaffia, Sweden and Lapland. London, 1723, fol. II vol.

The fame in French; A la Haye, 1727. *fol.* II; vol.

NEUVILLE EN HEZ.(ADRIAN BAILLET DE LA) Relation nouvelle & curieufe de Mofcovic contenant l'état prefent de cet empire; les expeditions des Mofcovites en Crimée en 1689, &c. A Paris, 1698. 12mo. do. à la Haye 1699, 12mo.

TOTT (BARON DE) *vide* CONSTANTINOPLE.

TOUNMANN (JEAN) Defcription de la Crimée, traduite de l'Allemand. A Strafbourg, 1786, 8vo.

CROATIA.

MOLL's Reife nach Croatien; in Bernoulli's Sammlung 14 ten Band, *vide* AUSTRIA.

POCOCKE (RICH.) *vide* ARCHIPELAGO.

WELSCHEN (HIERON) *vide* ARCHIPELAGO.

CUMBERLAND.

NICHOLSON (JOSHUA) and BURN's (RICH.) Hiftory and antiquities of the counties of Weftmoreland and Cumberland. London, 1777, gr. 4to. II vol.

ROBISON's (THOM.) Effay towards a natural hiftory of Cumberland and Weftmoreland, 1709, 8vo.

CYPRUS.

BRUYN (CORN. DE) Voyage au Levant, &c. A Delft, 1700, fol. A Paris, 1714, fol. do, à Paris & Rouen, 1725, 4to. II tom.
The fame in Dutch. Delft, 1609, fol.

DAPPER, *vide* ARCHIPELAGO.

HACKLUYT (RICH.) *vide* ANGLESEY.

HOPKEN OCH CARLSON, Twärna ftora fwenfka Heeres- refbefkrifning ifrän Cypern, til Afien, Jerufalem, &c. Stockholm, 1768.

MARITI (GIOV.) Viaggi per l' ifola di Cipro, per la Siria, e Paleftina. In Torino, 1769, 8vo. V vol. do. in Lucca, 1769; 8vo. tom. 1; do. in Firenze, 1769 & 1770; tom. II, V.

MARITI (JOH.) Reifen durch Cypern, Sirien, und

und Paleſtina von 1760 bis 1768. In einem
Aufzuge des 1ſten bis 5ten Bands von Chriſt.
Heinr. Haſe. Altenburg, 1777, 8vo.
PIACENZA (FRANC.) *vide* ARCHIPELAGO.
POCOCKE (RICH.) *vide* Do.
Sammlung der beſten und neueſten Reiſebe-
ſchreibungen in einem Aufzug. Berlin,
1765, 1782, 8vo. XXIII Bände.
SOMMER (JAN.) *vide* ARCHIPELAGO.

CZIRKNITZ (LAKE OF)

STEINBERG's (FRAN. ANT. VON) Gründliche
Nachricht von dem im innern Crain lie-
genden Czirknitzer See. Glatz, 1761, 4to.
mit 35 Kupfern.
WERNERI, Tabella lacus mirabilis ad Czirk-
nitz. Colon. 1595, fol.

DALMATIA.

BLOUNT's (HENRY) Voyage into the Levant,
London, 1634, 1737. 4to.
———————— Morgenländiſche Reiſe durch Dal-
matien, & Sclavonien, Thracien und Egypten. Helmſtadt, 1678, 4to.
FORTIS (ALB) Viaggio in Dalmazia. In Venezia, 1774, 4to. II tom.

The

. *The same into German.* Bern, 1776, 8vo. *II Bände.*
The same into French, translated from the Italian. Bern, 1787, 8vo. *II tom.*

———————— Travels into Dalmatia, in a series of letters, &c. with remarks on the isle of Cherso & Osero. London, 1778, 4to.

———————— Sitten der Morlaken, ein Auszug aus dessen Reisen nach Dalmatia. Bern, 1775. 8vo.

FABRI's (JOH. ERNST.) Sammlung von Stadt, Land, und Reise Beschreibungen. Halle, 1783, gr. 8vo.

LOURICH (GIOV.) Osservazioni sopra diversi pezzi del viaggio in Dalmazia del Abate Fortis. In Venezia, 1776, 4to.

———————— Lettera apologetica al Sig. Ant. Lorgna, in cui si confutano varie censure fatte alle sue osservazioni sopra diversi pezzi del viaggio del Abate Fortis. In Padua 1776, 4to.

NUTRIZIO GRISOGONO (PIETRO) Notizia per servire alla storia naturale della Dalmazia con l' aggiunta di un compendio della storia civile del Signor Giov. Rossignoli. In Trevigi, 1780, 4to.

ROBERT's Voyage to Dalmatia in Hackluyt (Rich.) *vide* ANGLESEY.

SCALMER (PIETRO) Sermone parenetico al Sig. Giov. Lourich. In Modena, 1776, 4to.

SPON

SPON & WHEELER, Voyages d' Italie, de Dalmatie, de la Grece, &c. A Lyon, 1678, gr. 12mo. II vol. do. A Amsterdam 1679, gr. 12mo. III vol. A la Haye, 1714, 8vo. II vol.
The same translated into Italian by Frefchot. In Bologna, 1688, 12mo. II tom.
The same in German. Nurnberg, 1690, 1713, fo. II Theile.
VILLA (MARCH. GHIR. FRANC.) Viaggi in Dalmazia e Levante. In Torino, 1668, 4to.
WHEELER (GEORGE) Voyage de Dalmatie, de la Grece, & du Levant. A Utrecht, 1682, 12mo. A Amsterdam, 1689, gr. 12mo. II tom. A la Haye, 1723. 8vo. II tom.
---------- Journey into Dalmatia, Greece, and the Levant. London, 1682, fol.

DANUBE RIVER.

MARSILII (ALOYS. FERD. COMITIS) Danubius Pannonico --- Myficus, obfervationibus geographicis, aftronomicis, hydrographicis, hiftoricis, phyficis, perluftratus. Hagaé Comitis & Amfterdam, 1726, fol. VI tom.
F. (J. F.) Die Donau Reife, *vide* CONSTANTINOPLE.

DAU-

DAUPHINÉ.

FAUJAS DE ST. FOND Histoire naturelle de la province du Dauphiné. A Grenoble & Paris, 1781, 4to. tom I.

GIRAUD SOULAVIE vide AUVERGNE.

DENMARK.

ADAM'S (MELCH.) Beschrivning om Swerige, Danmark, och Norige, af Joh. Fred. Peringskiöld, 1718, 4to.

Anecdoten eines Reisenden Russen uber die Staats Verfassung, Sitten, und Gebräuche, in Briefen an seine Freunde. Lubeck, 1771, 8vo.

AUBERY (DE MAURIER) Memoires de Hambourg, de Lubeck, de Holstein, de Danemarc, de Suede & de Pologne. A la Haye, 1737, 8vo.

BERNHARD (ARNOLD) Danemarkes og Norges frugtbare herlighed. Kiopenh. 1656, 4to.

BERNOULLI'S ARCHIV. vide BELLUNO, & AUSTRIA.

CARLISLE (COMTE DE) Relation de trois Ambassadeurs de la part du Roi de la Grande Bretagne, Charles IId. vers Alexey Michaelowitz

Chaclowitz Czar, Charles II Roi de Suede, & Frederic III Roi de Danemarc en l' année 1665, traduit de l' Anglois. A Amfterdam, 1700, 12mo.

The fame in German. Frankfurt & Leipzig. 1704, 12mo.

COXE's (WILL.) Travels into Poland, Ruffia, Sweden and Denmark. London, 1784, 4to. II vol.

———— *Tranflated into German.* Zurch, 1784, 1785, 4to. II Bände.

Dänemark mit einer ausfuhrlichen Befchreibung. Kopenhagen, 1746, 3 Theile, fol. mit 281 Karten.

GOETCERI's (ANT.) Journal der legatie gedaen in de jaaren 1615, 1616 van weegen Haare Hoogmogende aan de Koninghen van Sweden ende Denmark ende den Keyfer van Rufchland. Gravenhage, 1619, 4to.

HAYES DE COURMESUIN (DES) Voyage en Danemarc enrichi d' annotations par le Sieur (P. M.) L. A Paris, 1664, 12mo.

HEBERER VON BRETTEN (MICH.) Befchreibung feiner dreyjährigen Dienftbarkeit, und nachherigen Reifen in Böhmen, Pohlen, Sweden, Denmark, &c. Heidelberg, 1610, 4to.

HERMANNIDAE (RUTGERI) Defcriptio Daniae et Norwegiae. Amfter. 1670, 12mo. II tom.

———— Deliciae five amoenitates Daniae-Norwegiae,

Norwegiae, Slefwici, Holfatiae. Lugd. Bat.
1706, 12mo. II tom.
HOLK (H.) Reyfe Wegwifer i Danemark og Holfteen, 2te Oplage. Kiobenh. 1780, 12mo.
HONTAN (DE LA) Suite du voyage &c. avec les voyages en Portugal & en Danemarc. A Amfterdam, 1704, 12mo.
The fame in German. Hamburg & Leipzig. 1711, 12mo.
Iftoria naturale, morale, e politica della Mofcovia, di Suecia, di Danemarca, di Norwegia, e della Groenlandia. In Venezia, 1738, 8vo.
Letters from an Englifh gentleman on his travels through Denmark, 1773. London, 8vo.
Lettres fur le Danemarc. A Copenhague, 1763, 1764.
LOMENII Itinerarium, *vide* AUSTRIA.
MALGO'S KING OF BRITAIN Voyage to Ifland, Gothland, Orkney, Denmark, & Norway, in Hackluyt's principal navigations. *vide* ANGLESEY.
MARSHALL's Travels through Holland, Flanders, Germany, Denmark, Sweden, Lapland, Ruffia, Ukrain, Poland, &c. London, 1772, gr. 8vo. III vol.
The fame in German. Dantzig, 1773, 1775, 8vo. *III Theile.*
---------- Voyage dans la partie Septentri, onale.

onale de l' Europe. A Paris, 1776, 8vo. III tom.

OCTHER'S Voyage into the Sound of Denmark, & WALSTAN'S navigation into the Sound of Denmark. In Hackluyts principal navigations. *vide* ANGLESEY.

OGERI (CAROLI) Ephemerides, five iter Danicum, Succicum, & Polonicum. Lut. Paris. 1656, 8vo.

PAYEN VOYAGES &c. *vide* BRABANT.

PONTOPPIDAN'S (ERICH.) Theatrum Daniae Veteris & modernae; oder Schaubuhne des alten und jetzigen Dännemarks. Bremen, 1730, 4to.

---------- Danske Atlas. Kiobenh, 1763, V dele.

---------- Beschreibung des Königreich's Dännemark nach seinen politischen und physicalischen Beschaffenheiten. Copenhagen & Hamburg, 1765, 1767; gr. 4to. II Theile.

RATHGEBEN'S (JACOB) & SCHICKHARD VON HERRENBERG (HEINRICH) Beschreibung zweyer Reisen Herzog Fridrichs von Wurtenberg durch Deutschland, Dännemark, & Ungarn; auch in Italien und nachher in Engelland. Herausgegeben von Allius. Tubingen 1604. 4. Holzschn.

RANDOLPH'S Observations of the present state of Denmark, Russia and Switzerland in a
series

feries of letters. London, 1784, gr. 8vo.

REGNARD, Voyages de Flandre, d' Hollande, de Suede, Danemarc, Lapponie, Pologne, & Allemagne. A Rouen, 1731, 8vo. V tom.

Reife-veivifer i Danmark og Holfteen. Kiobenh. 1780. 8vo.

ROGER, Lettres fur le Danemarc. A Geneve 1757, 8vo. augmentées d' un fecond tome par Sam. Francois Reverdil. A Geneve 1765, 8vo. II tom.

The fame in German. Copenhagen, 1758, gr. 8vo.

SCHEEL (HEINR. OTTO) Almindelig udkaft af kriegers fkueplads: ellèr geographifk, topographifk och hiftorifk befkrivelfe Kongerigerne Danmark, Norge, og Swerig, famt deres Tydfke provindfen fom Tadledning til Kong Friedrick IV Krigs hiftorie. Krob. 1785, 4to.

SCHLEGELS (JOH. HEIN.) Dänifche Reifebefchreibungen, aus der Sammlung zur Danifchen Gefchichte uberfetzt. Kopenhagen, 1776, 8vo.

SCHYTTE (ANDR.) Danemarks og Norges naturlige og politifke Toefatning. Kiob. 1777, 8vo. Forfte deel.

---------- Dänemarks & Norwegens natuiliche und politifche Verfaffung aus dem Dänifchen ins Deutfche uberfetzt; mit Zufätzungen und gutten Anmerkungen. Flenfburg und Leipzig, 1782. 8vo. 1ter. Theil.

VERDUN

VERDUN'S (ULRICH VON) Reifen durch Frankreich, Engelland, Dänemark, und Sweden von 1670—1677, in Bernoulli's Archiv zur neuen Gefchichte &c. 6ter Theil Leipzig, 1787, gr. 8vo.

VERNON (DU) Relation en forme de journal de voyage fait en Danemarc à la fuite de Mr. l' Ambaffadeur d' Angleterre. A Rotterdam 1706, 8vo. Do. 1710, 12mo. II vol.

-------- Travels through Denmark. London, 1707, 8vo.

---------- Viaggio d'un uomo qualificato, *vide*, ENGLAND.

WILLIAMS'S (T.) Rife, progrefs, and ftate of the northern governments, viz. the United Provinces, Denmark, Sweden, Ruffia, and Poland. London, 1777, 4to. II vol.

The fame tranflated into German. Leipzig, 1779, 1780, 8vo. *II Th.*

ZEILLER'S (MART.) Befchreibung des Königreich's Dänemark und Norwegen. Ulm. 1648, 1658, 8vo.

------- Defcriptio regnorum Daniae & Norwegiae, nec non ducatuum Slefvici & Holfatiae. Amfterdam, 1655, 12mo. cum tab. aeneis.

DER

DERBYSHIRE.

BERNOULLI, *vide* AUSTRIA.
FERBER's (J. J.) Verſuch einer Oryktographie von Derbyſhire in England auf einer Reiſe dahin. Mietau, 1776, 8vo.
LEICH (CHARLES) *vide* CHESHIRE.
Sketch of a tour into Derbyſhire, *vide* BEDFORDSHIRE.

DEVONSHIRE.

RISDON's (THOM.) Chorographical deſcription of Devonſhire. London, 1713, 8vo.

DORSETSHIRE.

COKER's Survey of Dorſetſhire, containing the antiquities and natural hiſtory of that county. London, 1732, fol.
HUTCHIN's hiſtory and antiquities of the county of Dorſet.

DRESDEN.

BUCHER's (URBAN GOTT.) Sachſenlandes Natur Hiſtorie, &c. Dreſden & Pirna, 1723 & 1727, 8vo.

KINDLEBEN (CHRIST. WILH.) UNTER DEM NAHMEN HARTENSTEIN Reife von Berlin, über Roftock nach Drefden. Hall, 1780, 8vo.
Neue Reife-Bemerkungen in und über Deutfchland, *vide* BERLIN.
Reife im Sommer, 1780, *vide* BERLIN.
Reife von Wien uber Prag, *vide* Do.
SHERLOCK's (MART.) *vide* Do.
ZURNER's (ADAM FRID.) Anleitung zur Reife von Drefden nach Warfchau. Nurnberg, 1738, 12mo.

DUBLIN.

A month's tour in North Wales, Dublin, and its environs. London, 1781.

DURHAM.

WALLIS's (JOHN) Natural Hiftory and Antiquities of Northumberland. London, 1769, gr. 4to. II vol.

EDINBURG.

SULIVAN's (RICH. JOS.) Tour through part of England, Scotland and Wales in 1778, London

London, 1780, 8vo. Do. 1785, 8vo. II vol.

TOPHAM's (E.) Letters from Edinburgh, written in the years 1774 and 1775. London, 1776, 8vo.

The fame tranflated into German. Leipzig, 1777, 8vo.

EISENACH.

VOIGT's (JOH. CARL. WITH.) Mineralogifche Reifen durch das Hertzogthum Weimar und Eifenach. Weimar, 1785, gr. 8vo.

ELBA.

KOESTLIN (C. H.) Lettres fur l'hiftoire naturelle de l'ifle d'Elbe. A Vienne, 1780, 8vo.

ENGLAND.

A new difplay of the Beauties of England: a defcription of the moft elegant public edifices, royal palaces, noblemen's and gentlemen's feats, and other curiofities natural and artificial, by a fociety of gentlemen

tlemen, revifed by (P.) Ruffel. London, 1769, fol. III edit. London, 1776, 8vo. II vol.

An account of the character and manners of the French, with occafional obfervations on the Englifh. London, 1770, 8vo. II vol.

A tour through the whole ifland of Great Britain, divided into circuits. London, 1738, 12mo. III vol. 1743. Do. 1755. Ditto 1769. Do. 1778, 8vo. IV vol.

A journey through part of England and Scotland. London, 1746, 8vo.

A journey through England and Scotland. London, 1722, 8vo. 3 vol.

ALBERTIS (GEORG WILH.) Briefe betreffend den allerneueften Zuftand der Religion und Wiffenfchaften in Grofs Brittannien. Hannover, 1752, 1754, 8vo. IV Th.

ANGELONI's Letters on the Englifh nation, tranflated from the Italian. Lond. 1755, 8vo. II vol.

ANTONINI AUGUSTI Iter Brittaniarum commentariis (J. H.) Gali illuftratum. Revifit, auxit, edidit Robert Gale filius.— Accedit Antonii Ravennatis Brittanniae chorographia. Londini, 1709, 4to.

ARCHENHOLZ (T. W. VON) England und Italien. Leipzig, 1785, 8vo. II Bände.

Die 2te. Aufgabe, Leipzig, 1787, 8vo. V Th.

BARETTI (JOS) Journey from London to Genoa, through England, Portugal, Spain, and France. London, 1770, 8vo. IV vol.

The fame tranflated into German. Leipzig, 1772, 8vo. II Th.

The fame in French, Amfterdam, 1776, 8vo. IV vol.

BEVERELL (JAMES) Delices de la Grande Bretagne & d'Irlande. A Leide, 1707, Do. 1727, 12mo. VIII vol.

BERKENHOUT'S (JOH) Outlines of the natural hiftory of Great Britain and Ireland. London, 1769, 1771, 8vo. III vol.

BERNOULLI *vide* AUSTRIA.

BERNOULLI'S SAMMLUNG, 13 BAND, *vide* AUSTRIA.

Befchreibung von Grofs Brittannien, nebft einer Gefchichte der Grofbrittannifchen Schiffahrt. Aus dem Englifchen, 1780, 8vo.

Befchreibung einer Reife aus Deutfchland durch einen Theil von Frankreich, England, und Holland. Breflau, 1783, 8vo. II Th.

BJOERNSTAEHL (JAC JON.) refa dil Frankrike, Italien, Schweitz, Tyfkland, Holland, England, Turkiet, och Grekland efter des Töd utgifven af (C. C.) Gjözwell* Sjette Delen. Stockh. 1784, 4to.

The fame, vide CONSTANTINOPLE.

BLANC (L'ABBE, LE) Sur le genie, les moeurs, & le gouvernement des Anglois, & des François. A Lyon, 1758, 12mo. III vol.

BOCCAGE (MAD. DE) Lettres concernant fes voyages en France, en Angleterre, en Hollande, & en Italie. Drefden, 1771, 8vo.

BOSC (NIC.) Voyage pour negocier la paix entre les couronnes de France, & d'Angleterre en 1381. Joint aux voyages litteraires de Martene (Edw.) & Durant (Urfin) A Paris, 1717, 1724, gr. 4to. II vol. *vide* FRANCE.

BRAZEY (M. DE) Guide d'Angleterre. Paris & Amfterdam, 1744, 8vo.

Briefe über den gegenwärtigen Zuftand von Engelland, befonders in Anfehung der Politick, der Künfte, der Sitten, und fchoenen Wiffenfchaften. Aus dem Englifchen. Leipzig, 1777, 8vo.

BROME's (JAMES) Travels in England, Scotland, and Wales. London, 1700, 8vo. The fecond edition, with large additions. London, 1707, 8vo.

BURTON's (WILL.) commentary on the itinerary of Antoninus, fo far as it concerned Brittain. London, 1758, fol.

BUSCH's (JOH. GEORG.) Bemerkungen auf einer Reife durch die vereinigten Niederlanden und England. Hamburg, 1786, gr. 8vo. Sind auch enthalten im VIIIten Band der neuen Sammlung von Reisebeschreibungen.—Die erften V Bände find herausgekommen in Hamburg, 1780, 1783, gr. 8vo.

BUSCHEL (C.) Neue Reife eines Deutfchen nach England im Jahr, 1783. Ein Pendant zu des H. P. Moriz Reife. Berlin, 1784. 8vo.

B. (R.) Admirable curiofities, rarities, and wonders in England, Scotland and Ireland. London, 1684, 3vo.

CAMPBELL's (JOHN) Political Survey of G. B. London, 1774, gr. 4to. II vol.

CELLIUS (EBRH.) Befchreibnng zweyer Reifen, welche H. Fridrich von Wurtenberg durch England, und die Niederlande, 1592, imgleichen nach Italien im Jahr, 1599 gethan. Tubingen, 1603, 1604, 4to.

CHILDRY (J.) Britannia Baconica. London, 1661. 8vo.

The fame tranflated into French. A Paris, 1677, 12mo.

Confiderations on the police, commerce, and circumftances of the Kingdom of England, London, 1771, 8vo.

CORONELLI (P.) Viaggi nell' Inghilterra. In Venezia, 1697, 8vo. IV tom.

COULON.

Coulon (Louis) Fidele conducteur pour le voyage d'Angleterre. A Paris, 1654, 8vo.

Coyer (Abbe) Nouvelles observations sur l' Angleterre. A Paris, 1779. 8vo.

The same translated into German. Gotha, 1781, 8vo.

Deichsel's Reise nach Holland und Engelland, in Bernoulli's Archiv. *vide* Belluno.

Description of all the Counties in England and Wales. London, 1736, 8vo.

Die Flucht eines Franzosen nach England, oder Bemerkungen über den Character und Gebräuche der Englischen Nation. Franckfurt und Leipzig. 1780, 8vo.

Drayton's (Mich.) Polyalbion. London, 1658, fol.

Ebert (Adam) unter dem nahmen Aulus Apronius Reisebeschreibungen von Villa Franca durch Deutschland, Holland, Engelland, Frankreich, Spanien und Italien. Franckfurt an der Oder 1723, 8vo. Ditto, 1724, 8vo.

Eisenbergii (Petri) itinerarium Galliae & Angliae (Deutsch) Leipzig, 1614, 1623, 12mo.

Elveri (Hier.) deliciae apodemicae. Lips. 1611, 8vo.

England illustrated, or a compendium of the natural history, geography, topography and

and antiquities ecclefiaftical and civil of England and Wales. London. 1764, 4to. 2 vol.

ENS (CASP.) Deliciae Magnae Brittanniae. Colon, 1613, 8vo.

ERNDEL (CHRIST. HENR.) De itinere fuo Anglicano & Batavo 1706 & 1707 facto relatio ad amicum, qua variae ad anatomiam, chirurgiam, botanicam & materiam medicam fpectantes obfervationes fiftuntur. Amftelod. 1710, 1711, 8vo.

Etat abregé des loix, revenus, ufages & productions de la grande Bretagne. A Londres, 1757, 8vo.

FERBER (JOH. JAC). *vide* BOHEMIA.

FERDINAND ALBRECHT HERZOG VON BRAUNSWEIG BEVERN DES WUNDERLICHEN wunderliche Begebenheiten und Reifebefchreibung durch Deutfchland, Italien, Malta, Frankreich und England. Bevern, 1678, 1680, 4to. II Theile.

FORSTER (JEAN REIN.) Tableau d' Angleterre l' année 1780, continué jufqu à l' année, 1783.

The fame tranflated into German. Deffau, 1784, 8vo.

GORDON's (ALEXAND.) itinerarium Septentrionale. London 1726, fol. with 66 charts.

GRAM (CHRISTEN) Kort journal eller Reifebefchrivelfe til England. Chriftiania, 1760, 4to.

GRASSERI

GRASSERI (JOH. JAC·) Volkommene Italiänifche, Französifche, und Englifche Schatzkammer, IX B. Bafel 1609, 8vo.

GRIM (JOH. FR. CARL.) Bemerkungen eines Reifenden durch Deutfchland, Frankreich, Engelland und Holland. Altenburg, 1775, 8vo. III Theile.

GROSLEY Londres: à Lauffanne. Paris 1768, 1770, 12mo, III tom. augmenté de notes d'un Anglois. A Neufchatel, 1771, 12mo. III tom.

GAULANDRI'S (ANGELO) Lettere odoporiche di Francia, Inghilterra, &c. In Venez. 1780.

GUINDERODA (FR. JUST. VON) Befchreibung einer Reife aus Deutfchland durch einige Theile von Frankreich, England, und Holland. Breflau, 1783, 8vo. 2 Th.

HACKLUYT (RICHARD) vide ANGLESEY.

HENZNERI (PAUL) itinerarium Germaniae, Galliae, Angliae, & Italiae. Norimbergae, 1612, 8vo. Do. 1629, 8vo.

HERMANNIDAE (RUTGERI) Brittannia Magna. Amftel, 1661. 12mo.

HERVEY'S (FRED.) naval hiftory of Great Britain, from the earlieft times to the rifing of the Parliament. Lond. 1779, 8vo. vol.

HOCHSTETTER (AND. ADAM) oratio de utilitate peregrinationis Anglicanae. Tub. 1697, 4to.

HOEN

HOEN (GEORG PAUL) iter juridicum, quod jurium culter per Belgium, Angliam, Galliam, & Italiam jucunda cum utilitate inftituere poteft. Witteb. 1688, 12mo.

H. (COMTE F. DE) Lettres fur la France, l' Angleterre & l'Italie. A Geneve, 1785, 8vo.

HARTIG (GRAF F. VON) intereffante Briefe über Frankreich, England, und Italien. Eifenach, 1786, 8vo.

HOGREWE'S (JOH. LUD.) Befchreibung der in Engelland feit 1759 angelegten und jetzt größtentheils vollendeten fchiffbaren Kanäle, zur innern Gemeinfchaft der vornehmften Handels-Städte. Nebft einem Verfuch einer Gefchichte der inländifchen Schiffahrt und aller bis ietzt in—und aufferhalb Europa bekannten fchiffbahren Canälen. Hannover, 1780, gr. 4to.

JARS (JABR.) Voyages metallurgiques, ou recherches, & obfervations fur les mines & forges de fer, la fabrication d'acier, celle du fer blanc, & plufieurs mines de Charbon de terre, les mines d'or & d' argent, celles de plomb, de cuivre, de bifmuth, de cobalt, & de mercure ; les fabriques d'azure, de cerufe, du blanc de plomb, & du minium; fur les mines de calamine d'étain; les mines & fabriques d'alun, de foufre, & de vitriol, &c. faites depuis, 1757 jufqu'a 1769 en Allemagne,

Suede,

Suede, Norvege, Angleterre, Ecoffe, &c. A Lyon, 1774. 4to. tom. I. A Paris, 1780, 1781, 4to. tom. II & III.

The fame tranflated into German. Berlin, 1777, gr. 8vo. II Bände.

Journey through England and Scotland. London, 1714, 8vo. III vol.

Journey through England along with the army, 1747, 8vo.

JORDAN (CH. ETIENNE) hiftoire d'un voyage litteraire de l'an 1733, en France, en Angleterre, & en Hollande, A la Haye, 1735, 12mo.

JOVII (PAUL) defcriptio Britanniae, Scotiae, Hiberniae. & Orcadum. Bafil, 1546.

KALM (PEHR) refa til Norra America, &c. Stockh. 1753, 1756, 1761, 8vo. III Delar.

The fame tranflated into German, by Murray. Göttingen, 1754, 1757, 1764, 8vo. III Bände.

The fame tranflated into Englifh, by Förfter. London, 1771, 8vo. III vol.

The fame tranflated into Dutch. Utrecht, 1772, 4to. II Deele.

KIRCHMAIER (GEORG CASP) de Anglici regni genio, moribus, ac dotibus. Wittenb. 1682, 4to.

KUECHELBECKER (JOH. BASIL) Der nach

L En-

Engelland reifende curiöfe Paffagier. Hannover, 1726, Do. 1736, 8vo.

Lettres curieufes de voyage ecrites d'Angleterre, d'Italie, d'Hongrie, & d'Allemagne. A Paris, 1691, 8vo.

LELAND's (JOHN) itinerary of Great Britain. London, 1710, 1712, 8vo. IX vol.

Le guide d'Angleterre, ou relation curieufe du voyage de Monfr. de B***. A Amfterdam, 1744, 8vo.

LOCHNERI (JAC. HIER) obfervationes Anglicae. Bremae, 1714, 4to.

L. (C. F. H.) Reife-Bemerkungen über einen Theil von Italien, Frankreich, und England, nebft einem Anhang von Algier. Celle, 1784, 8vo.

M. (C. P. D.) Relation des voyages en Allemagne, Angleterre, Hollande, Boheme, & Suiffe. A Rouen, 1676, 12mo.

MARTIN's (BENJ.) natural hiftory of England and Wales. London, 1704, 8vo. II vol. Do. 1759, 8vo. II vol.

MISSON's (MAR.) memoirs and obfervations in his travels over England, and fome account of Scotland and Ireland. London, 1719, 8vo.

MOLL's (HERM) new defcription of England and Wales. London.

MONCONYS, *vide* CONSTANTINOPLE.

MORITS

MORITZ (CARL PHIL.) Reife eines Deutfchen nach England im Jahr 1782. Berlin, 1783, 8vo.

Anmerkungen und Erinnerungen uber H. P. Moritz Briefe aus England von einem Deutfchen, der auch einmal in England gewefen ift. Göttingen, 1785, 8vo.

MURALT lettres fur les Anglois & les François, 1725, 1728.

The fame tranflated into German. Weimar, 1761, 8vo.

MYLIUS Reife von Berlin nach England in Bernoulli's Archiv *vide* BELLUNO.

NEUMAIR VON RAMSLA (JOH. WILH) Befchreibung der Reife, welche Johan Ernft der jungere Herzog von Sachfen in Frankreich, England, und Niederland. 1613, 1614, hinterleget. Leipzig, 1620, 4to.

NIVEL (H.) Voyage forcé, ou maniere de tirer avantage des circonftances, tiré des memoires d'un homme de lettres, qui a fait un long fejour en Angleterre, & en a obfervé les moeurs, et les ufages. A Paris, 1779, 12mo.

NORDEN's fpeculi Britanniae pars. London, 1723, 4to.

Nouvelles obfervations fur l'Angleterre par un voyageur. A Paris, 1779, 12mo.

Nouvel itineraire general, comprenant toutes les grandes routes & chemins de communication

nication des provinces de France, des isles Brittanniques, d' Espagne, de Portugal, d' Italie, &c. A Paris, 1776, gr. 4to. II tom.

Observations d'un gentilhomme Anglois, avec quelques lettres sur la relation de Mr. Sorbiere, & l'arret du Conseil, qui ordonne la suppression de la dite relation. A Paris, 1664, 12mo.

Observations made during a tour through parts of England, Scotland, and Wales. London, 1779, 4to.

Translated into German, with an additional description of Yorkshire. Leipzig, 1781, 8vo.

OEDER's (JOH. LUD) Beyträge zur Oeconomie, Cameral, und Policey Wissenschaft, aus dessen Berichten von seinen Reisen nach der Schweitz, Holland, Frankreich, und England im Jahr 1759 & 1763. Dessau, 1782, 8vo.

OGILBI's (JEAN) itineraire de toutes les routes de l'Angleterre. A Paris, 1759, 4to. avec CI cartes par Sener.

OWEN's (JAMES) Britannia depicta. London, 1756, 4to. CCXXXVII charts.

PATIN (CHARLES) *vide* BOHEMIA.

PAYEN, *vide* BRABANT.

Present state of the nation of Great Britain, respecting it's trade, finances, &c. London, 1769, gr. 8vo.

RATHGEBEN'S (JACOB) kurtze und wahrhafte Befchreibung der Badenfahrt, welche Herzog Fridrich zu Wurtenberg im Jahr 1592 von Mümpelgard aus in England, und durch die Niederlanden zurück nach Mumpelgard verichtet hat. Tubingen, 1602, 4to.

RATHGEBEN (JACOB) UND SCHICKHARD VON HERRENBERG (HEINRICH) *vide* DENMARK.

Reife-Befchreibung nach Spanien und England aus dem Franzöfifchen überfetzt durch Johan Mackle. Frankfurt, 1667, 12mo.

Reife-magazin, Altona, 1784, 8vo. I Band in 3 Stücken.

Reifbefchryvinge door Vrankryk, Spanje, Italien, Duytfland, England, Holland, Mofkovien, &c. Leiden, 1700, 4to.

Reifen und Begebenheiten in Frankreich, Italien, Deutfchland, Holland und Engelland eines Cavaliers im Dienft Guftav. Adolphs König in Sweden, und Karls I. K. in England; heraufgegeben von (Dan) Defse. Leipzig, 1785, 8vo. II Th.

Reponfe aux fauffetés & invectives de la relation de Mr. Sorbiere. A Amfterdam, 1675, 12mo.

RICHARD's character of the Englifh nation by a French Pen. London, 1771, 8vo.

RODEN (VON) denkwürdige Reifen Johan
. Lim-

Limbergs durch Deutschland, Italien, Spanien, Portugal, England, Frankreich und Schweitz. Leipzig 1690, 12mo.

ROGER's hiſtorical account of three years travels over England and Wales. London, 1694, 8vo.

ROHAN (DUC DE) voyage fait en 1600 en Italie, Allemagne, Païs Bas, Angleterre, & Ecoſſe. A Amſterdam, 1646, 12mo.

ROSMITAL & BLATNA (LEONIS L. B. DE) commentarius brevis itineris anno 1565, 1566 per Germaniam, Belgium, Angliam, Hiſpaniam, & Italiam facti; ex Bohemica in linguam Latinam tranſlatus. Olomuci, 1577, 8vo.

R. (LE B. DE) Lettres ſur un voyage fait dans quelques provinces meridionales de l'Angleterre. A Dreſde, 1786.

SAGITTARII (THOM) Ulyſſes Saxonicus, ſeu Iter Johannis Erneſti Ducis Saxoniae in Germaniam, Galliam, Angliam, & Belgium. Breſlaviae, 1621, 4to.

Sammlung der beſten und neueſten Reiſebeſchreibungen in einem Aufzug. Berlin, 1765, 1782, gr. 8vo. XXIII Bände.

SCHEID's (HIERONYMUS) Beſchreibung der Reiſe von Erfurt nach den Gelobten Lande, Spanien, Frankreich, England, und Holland. Erfurt, 1615, 1617, 4to. Helmſt, 1674, 1679, 4to.

SOR-

SORBIERE (SAM) relation d'un voyage en Angleterre. A Paris. 1664, 12mo. A Cologne, 1666 & 1669 12mo.

The same translated into English with Thomas Spratt's observations on it. London, 1709, 8vo.

SPRAT (TH.) on Mr. Sorbiere's voyage into England. Savoye. 1668, 12mo.

SPRENGEL'S (M. C.) Geschichte der wichtigsten geographischen Entdeckungen durch Reisen. Hall, 1783, 8vo. nach 11 Völkern: den Phoniciern, Griechen, Römern, Arabern, Normännern, Portugiesen, Spaniern, Holländern, Engländern, Russen und den Pabst durch Missionarien; in 11 Abschnitten.

STUKELEY'S (WILL.) itinerarium curiosum, or an account of the antiquities and curiosities in nature and art, observed in travels through Great Britain. London. 1724, fol.

SULIVAN, vide EDINBURGH.

TAUBE (FRID. WILH. VON) Abschilderung der Englischen Manufacturen, Handlung, Schifffahrt, und Colonien nach ihrer jetzigen Beschaffenheit. Wienn, 1774. 8vo. Do. 1777.

The modern universal British Traveller. London, 1779, fol.

The

The Englifh topographer, or an hiftorical account of all the pieces that have been written relating to the antiquities, natural hiftory, and topographical defcriptions of any part of England. London, 1720, 8vo.

The new Britifh Traveller. London, 1784, fol.

Tour through Great Britain. London, 1753, 4to. VIII vol.

UFFENBACH (ZACH. CONR. VON) merkwürdige Reifen durch Nieder Saehfen, Holland, und England. Frankf. & Leipz. 1753 & 1754, gr. 8vo. III Th.

Viaggj d'un uomo qualificato, trad. dal Francefe da Guil. Cefare Laurenti. Torino, 1685, 12mo.

V. (H. M. DE) Memoires faits par un voyageur en Angleterre, avec une obfervation de ce qu'il y a de plus curieux à Londres. A la Haye, 1698, 12mo.

VOLKMANN's (J. J.) Reifen durch England, vorzüglich in Abficht auf Kunft—Sammlungen, Naturgefchichte, Oeconomie, Manufa&turen, und Landfitze der Groffen. Aus den beften Nachrichten und neuen Schriften zufammen getragen. Leipz. 1781, 8vo.

8vo. IV Bände.

Voyage philosophique d'Angleterre fait en 1683 & 1684. A Londres & à Paris, 1787, 8vo. II tom.

Wanderungen eines philosophischen Menschenfreundes in America und England. Luneburg, 1786, 8vo.

WATZDORF (H. VON) Brief zur Characteristick von England gehörig auf einer Reise im Jahr 1784. Leipzig, 1786, 8vo.

WENDEBORN'S (GEBH. FRID. AUG.) Beyträge zur Käntnüfs von Grofs Britannien. Lemgo, 1780, 8vo.

YOUNG's (ARTHUR) six weeks tour through the Southern counties of England and Wales. London, 1769, 8vo.

------- six months tour through the North of England, containing an account of the present state of agriculture, manufactures, and population, &c. London, 1769, IV vol.

The same translated into German. Leipzig, 1772, gr. 8vo. II Th.

------- Farmer's tour through the East of England. London, 1771. 8vo. IV vol.

The same translated into German. Leipzig, 1775, gr. 8vo. 3ter. & 4ter. Th.

YOUNG's (ARTHUR) observations on the present

sent state of the waste lands of Great Britain. London, 1773, 8vo.

ZEILLER's (M.) itinerarium Magnae Britanniae, Reisebeschreibung durch England, Schottland, und Irland. Strasburg, 1617, & 1674, 8vo.

ERINI SAINT.

RICHARD (FRANÇOIS) Relation de ce qui s'est passé de plus remarquable à St. Erini, isle de l'Archipel depuis l'êtablissement des P. P. Jesuites avec plusieurs choses memorables. A Paris, 1657, 8vo.

ERMENONVILLE.

A tour to Ermenonville, *vide* CHANTILLY.
MAIER's Reise nach Ermenonville, IN KLEINEN REISEN, *vide* COLOGNE.

EUROPE.

A REVIEW of the characters of the principal nations in Europe. London, 1670, 8vo. II vol.

ALBON

ALBON (GRAF VON) politifche, hiftorifche, und critifche Abbandlungen über die Regierungs Form einiger Reiche und Staaten von Europa. Aus dem Französifchen. Stettin, 1780, 1784, 8vo. II Bände.

ARTHUR'S (KING OF BRITAIN) voyage to Iceland and the moft North-eaftern quarters of Europe, Anno 517, contained in Hackluyt, vide ANGLESEY.

AVRIL (PHIL.) voyage en divers états d' Europe, & d' Afie, pour decouvrir un nouveau chemin à la Chine depuis 1685. 1691, A Paris 1691, 1692, 4to. do. 1693, 12mo. *The fame tranflated into German.* Hamburg, 1705, 8vo.

BENJAMINIS NAVARRENI FILII JONAE TUDELENSIS itinerarium, Hebraice cum Latina verfione; & notis atque praefatione (Conftantini) l' Empereur. Lugduni, 1633, 12mo. maj.

— — — — — — — Itinerarium, in quo res memorabiles, quas ante quadringentos annos, totum fere terrarum orbem (Galliam, Italiam, Graeciam Afiam, Aethiopiam, Arabiam, Siciliam, Germaniam, Bohemian, & Boruffiam) dimenfus vel ipfe vidit, vel a fide dignis fuae aetatis hominibus defcribuntur, interprete ARIA MONTANO. Antwerp. 1575, 8vo. do. 1585, 12mo. Subjectae funt defcriptiones Mechae & Medinae ex itinerario Vartomanni

manni & Wildii; praefixa vero differtatio, qnam fuae editioni praemifit Conft. l' Empereur, & nonnullae ejus notae. Helmftadii 1636, gr. 12mo, Lipfiae 1764, 8vo. *The fame tranflated into Englifh by B. Gerrans.* London, 1783, 12mo.

BLANC (VINCENT LE) vide ARCHIPELAGO.

BOCCOLARI (DOMIN.) nouvelle defcription de toutes le villes de l' Europe, & des chofes les plus remarquables, qu'il y a a voir dans chaque ville. A Avignon, 1780, 8vo.

BORDA (DE VERDUN DE LA CRENNE CHEVALIER DE) Voyage fait par ordre du Roi en 1771 & 1772 à quelques côtes d' Europe, d' Afrique & d' Amerique, pour corriger les cartes hydrographiques. Paris, 1779, 4to. II tom.

BOULLAYE LE GOUZ (CESAR EGASSE DE LA) Voyages & obfervations en Europe, Afie, & Afrique jufqu' en l' année 1650, 1653, 4to.

BREVAL (JOHN) vide ALSACE.

Briefe eines Reifenden Banditen uber Sklaverey, Möncherey, und Tyranney der Europaer. Leipzig, 1787, 8vo.

BRIEMLES (VINC.) Pilgerfahrt durch Europa, Afia, und Africa von 1707 bis 1725, mit Anmerkungen von Jo. Jos. Peck. Munchen, 1627, 4to. m. Karten.

BURCO (GIOV. BATT. DE) Viaggio di cirque anni

anni in Afia, Africa, ed Europa. Milano, 1686, 12mo.

CARLI (D.) Der nach Venedig überbrachte Mohr, oder Erzählung aller Denkwürdigkeiten, welche ihm in feiner Miſſion von 1666 bis 1685 in allen 4 Welttheilen, fonderlich in Ethiopien aufgeſtoſſen; aus dem Italienifchen. Augſburg, 1692, 4to.

CHANCEL's (A.) New journey over Europe, with obfervations. London, 1717, 8vo.

Charaﬅeriﬅic der vornehmſten Europaeifchen Nationen. Leipzig, 1778, 8vo.

CHYTRAEI (NATHAN) variorum in Europa itinerum deliciae, feu ex variis manufcriptis feleﬅiora tantum infcriptionum maxime-recentium monumenta. Bremae 1594, 1599, 1608, 8vo.

Compendium geographiae antiquae mappis d' Anvillianis XI majoribus accommodatum. Vol. I. Europam continentis pars poﬅerior. Norimb. 1785, 8vo.

COVALESCA, Defcrizione itineraria di varii paefi d' Europa, e di qualche luoghi di Africa fatta dall' anno 1765 fino a tutto il 1770. In Napoli 1771, 8vo.

CROME's (A. F. W.) Europen's Produﬅe, zum Gebrauch der neuen Produﬅen Karte von Europa. Deſſau, 1782, 8vo. Neue Auﬂage, Europens Produﬅe. Zweyter Verfuch. Hamburg 1784, 8vo 1ﬅer Theil, Portugal, Spanien,

Spanien, nebſt ihren Oſt und Weſt-Indiſchen Colonien.

– – – – – – – – – – über die Gröſſe und Bevölkerung der ſämmtlichen Europaeiſchen Staaten. Ein Beytrag zur Kenntniſs der Staaten-Verhältniſſe &c. &c. Leipzig 1786, 8vo. mit 1 groſſen Karte;

DUTENS itineraire des routes les plus frequentées. Londres, 1779, 8vo.

EGMOND, *vide* ARCHIPELAGO.

Etàt des cours de l'Europe, & des provinces de France, publié pour la premiere fois en 1783, par Mr. l'Abbé de la Roche Filhac. A Paris, 1787, T. I & II.

FARIA E SOUZA (M. DE) Europa Portugueſa, 2 edic. Liſboa, 1678, 1679, 1680, fol. 3 v.

F. B. Voyages hiſtoriques de l' Europe, augmentés du guide des voyageurs. A Amſterdam 1712, VIII tom.

FLACHAT (JEAN CLAUDE) Obſervations ſur le commerce, les arts, les metiers, l' economie, & les finances, faites pendant ſes voyages en Europe, Aſie, & Afrique. A Lyon, 1766, 12mo. II vol.

The ſame tranſlated into German. Leipzig, 1767 8vo. II. Th.

FURST (GEORG VON) Curiöſe Reiſen durch Europa. Sorau, 1739, 8vo.

GEMELLI CARRERI (GIOV. FRANC.) Viaggj di Europa. In Napoli, 1711, 8vo.

By

By the fame, Giro del mondo. In Venezia, 1719, 8vo. IX tom. In Napoli 1721, 8vo. IX tom.

The fame tranflated into French. A Paris, 1719, 1727, gr. 12mo. VI tom.

Handbuch der alten Erdbefchreibung zum Gebrauch der IX gröffern Danvillifchen Landcharten. Nurnberg 1786, 8vo. II Bände.

HOGREWE, *vide* ENGLAND.

HOGUET (DE LA) Nouvelles lettres galantes & hiftoriques fur divers fujets des voyages, qu'un gentilhomme François a fait en Europe. A Paris, 1691, 8vo.

JORDAN (C.) Voyages hiftoriques de l' Europe. A la Haye, 1692, 1701, 12mo. VIII vol. A Paris, 1695, 1702, 12mo. VIII vol. A Paris, 1721, 8vo. VIII vol. avec cartes.

Itineraire des routes les plus frequentées, ou journal d' un voyage aux villes principales.

KREBEL'S (GOTTFR.) vermehrte Europaeifche Reifen. Hamburg 1767, do. 1783, 8vo. II Theile.

Le voyageur politique en Europe. A Franckf. 1692, 1695, III tom. 8vo.

Letters of different parts of Europe and the Eaft written in the year 1750. They contain obfervations on the productions of nature, the monuments of arts, and the manners of inhabitants. London, 1753, 8vo. II vol.

LITGOW

Litgow (Will.) negentienjaarige landreis uyt Schottland, door Europa, Afia & Africa, uyt 't Engels. Amfterdam, 1652, 4to.

Mac Intosh, travels in Europe, Afia and Africa. London, 1782, 8vo. II vol.

The fame tranflated into German, with fome remarks. Leipzig, 1786, 8vo. II Bände.

May (Louis du) Prudent voyageur, contenant la defcription politique, de l' Afie, de l'Afrique, de l'Amerique, & particulierement de l' Europe. A Geneve, 1681, 1686, 12mo. III t.

Mayer's (Joh. Frid.) unter dem Nahmen Romani Landwirthfchaftliche Reifen durch die vornehmften Landfchaften Europens. Nurnberg, 1775, 1776, 1777, 1782, 8vo. IV Thiele.

Memoires inftructifs pour un voyageur dans les divers états de l' Europe, contenant des anecdotes propres a eclaircir l' hiftoire du tems; avec des remarques fur le commerce & l' hiftoire naturelle. Amfterdam, 1736, 1738, 12mo. II tom.

The fame tranflated into German. Berlin 1738, 8vo. II Theile.

Misselli il Burattino (Giuseppe) Ragguaglio veridico, overo iftruzzione per chi viaggia, colla defcrizzione di Europa. In Roma 1682, 12mo. Do. in Bologna 1699, 12mo. II tom.

The fame tranflated into German. Leipzig, 1687, 12mo.

MONCONYS *vide* CONSTANTINOPLE.

MONTAGUE (LADY MARY WORTLEY) London 1763, 12mo. II vol. Berlin, 1781, 8vo.

The fame tranflated into German. Leipzig, 1763, 8vo.

The fame additional volume, 1767, gr. 12mo.

The fame tranflated into German. Leipzig. 1767, 8vo.

The whole works tranflated into French by le P. Burnet. Amfterdam, 1763, 8vo. *Rotterdam,* 1764, 8vo. *Berlin,* 1764, 8vo.

MORYSON's (FINES) itinerary through different parts of Europe and Afia. London, 1617, 1619, fol. III vol.

MOTRAYE, *vide* CRIM.

------- Travels in feveral countries of ducal and royal Pruflia, Ruflia and Poland.

The fame in French, avec des remarques geographiques & topographiques faites en 1726. *Londres & Dublin,* 1732, *fo.*

MYLLER's (ANGELICUS MARIA) Befchreibung feiner fünf Reifen, die er in Europa, Afia, und Africa gethan, Wienn und Nurnberg, 1735, 4to.

NEITZSCHUTZ (GEORG. CHRIST. VON) Siebenjährige Weltbefchauung durch Europa, Afia und Africa, Bautzen 1666, 4 Nurnberg, 1673, 4to. Magdeburg, 1753, 4to.

N   Neuefte

Neuester Wegweiser durch ganz Europa. Berlin, 1787, 8vo.

Nogues, Voyages & avantures en Europe. A la Haye, 1728, 12mo. 1739, 12mo.

Nortleigh's (John) topographical descriptions, with histories and political observations made in two several voyages through most parts of Europe. 1702, 8vo.

The same translated into German. Amsterdam 1671, 4to.

Nugent's grand tour, containing a description of most of the cities, towns, and remarkable places of Europe. London, 1749, 8vo. IV vol.

Nouveau recueil de voyages au Nord de l' Europe, & de l' Asie, contenants les extraits de relations des voyages les plus estimés, & qui n' ont jamais été publiés en François. Ouvrage traduit de differentes langues, &c. A Paris 1785, 8vo. II tom.

Pacichelli (Giov. Batt) Memoria di viaggi per l' Europa Christiana. In Napoli 1685, 12mo. IV tom.

Peritsol (Abraham) itinera mundi sic dicta, nempe cosmographia Latina; versione donavit, & notas passim adjecit Thomas Hyde. Oxonii, 1691, 4to.

Petersdorff (Christoph.) itinerarium terrae Sanctae, & totius Europae. Erfurt 1616 8vo.

Pilati

PILATI (CHARLES ANT. DE) Voyages en differens païs de l' Europe en 1774, 1775, 1776, ou lettres ecrites de l' Allemagne, de la Suiffe, de l' Italie, de la Sicile, & de Paris. A la Haye, 1777, 8vo. II vol.

The fame tranflated into German. Leipzig. 1778, *8vo. II Theile.*

PINTO (FERNANDO MENDEZ) Peregrinaçam, en que da conta de muytas, e muyto eftranhas coufas, que vio, &c. Lifboa 1614, fol.

The fame tranflated into French by Bern. Fiquier. Paris, 1624. *Do.* 1645, *4to.*

The fame tranflated into Spanifh. En Valencia, 1645, *fol.*

The fame in Dutch. Amfterdam, 1653, *4to.*

The fame tranflated into German. Amfterdam, 1671, *4to.*

PÖLLNITZ, (CHARLES LOUIS DE) memoires contenants les obfervations qu'il a faites dans fes voyages en Europe. A Liege 1734, 12mo. III tom. A Londres, 1735, 8vo. III tom. A Amfterdam, 1735, gr. 12mo. III tom. A Amfterdam, 1737, 8vo. III tom.

————— Briefe, welche das merkwürdigfte feiner Reifen in fich enthalten. Frankfurt 1738, 8vo. III Theile.

————— Nouveaux memoires. Amfterdam, 1737, 8vo. II tom.

The fame memoirs in German. Frankfurt, 1789, II Th.

PRICE's (JOSEPH) travels in Europe, Afia, and Africa. London, 1782, 8vo.

Potamographia Europea cum Fiedleri fluminibus Germaniae. Ulmae, 1627, 12mo.

RAYNAL (GUIL. THOM.) Tableau de l' Europe pour fervir de Supplement à l' hiftoire philofophique & politique du commerce. Amfterdam 1774, gr. 8vo.

Reifealmanach für Europa. Wienn, 1773, 16mo.

Reifen in verfchiedene Länder von Europa, oder Briefe aus Deutfchland, der Schweitz, Italien, Sicilien, und Paris gefchrieben, 1778, 8vo. II Th.

Reifboek door de voornaamften koningryken & heerfchappyen van Europa. Amfterdam, 1729, gr. 12mo.

ROTH's (EBERH. RUD.) auferlefene Denkwurdïgkeiten von Europa. Ulm, 1749, 12mo.

SAILOR's letters written during his third voyage and travels in Europe, Afia, and America. London, 1766, 12mo. II vol.

SALMON's modern hiftory, or the prefent ftate of all nations. London, 1744, 1746. fol. III vol.

The fame tranflated into Italian. In Venezia, 1740, 1766, 8vo, XXVI vol.

The fame in French. Amfterdam, 1730.

The fame tranflated into German, with additions of M. Goch.

SCHUBART's (MICH.) Reife durch verfchiedene Länder von Europa. Coburg, 1708, fo.

SCHULTZ's (STEPHAN) Leitung des Höchften nach feinen Rath auf den Reifen durch Europa, Afia, und Africa. Hall, 1771, 1775, 8vo. V Th.

SEVERTII (FRANC) felectae Chriftiani orbis deliciae ex urbibus, templis, bibliothecis. Colon, 1625, 8vo.

SHERLOCK (MART.) *vide* BERLIN.

STRAHLENBERG (PHIL. JOH. VON) Nord und Oeftlicher Theil von Europa und Afia, &c. Leipzig, 1730, 4to.

SULIVAN's (R. T) *under the name* AKBAR OF BETLIS, philofophical rapfodies, containing reflexions on the laws, manners, cuftoms, and religions of certain Afiatic, African, and European nations. London, 1784, 1785, 8vo. III. vol.

The fame tranflated into German. Leipzig, 1787, 8vo. II Bände.

SULZER's (J.G.) Tagebuch einer von Berlin nach den mittäglichen Ländern von Europa, im Jahr 1775, und 1776 gethanen Reife und Zurückreife. Leipzig, 1780, 8vo.

The fame tranflated into French. A la Haye, 1782, gr. 8vo.

S. G. (G. R. FREYHERRN VON) Statiftifche Tabellen zur bequemen Uberficht der Größe,

Größe, Bevölkerung, des Reichthums und der Macht der vornehmsten Europeischen Staaten. Dritte vermehrte und verbesserte Auflage. Leipzig, 1786, gr. fol.

The American wanderer through various parts of Europe, by a Virginian. London, 1783, 8vo.

THEVENOT (N. M. DE) Voyages tant en Europe, qu'en Asie, & Afrique. A Paris, 1689, 8vo. V tom. Do. A Amsterdam, 1705, 1725, 12mo. V tom. Do. A Amsterdam, 1727, 8vo. V tom.

The same translated into German. Frankfurt, 1693, 4to. III Th.

TOZE, gegenwärtiger Zustand von Europa. Butzow, 1767, gr. 8vo. II Th. Dieses Werk ist umgearbeitet unter folgenden Titel erschienen: Einleitung zur allgemeinen, und besondern Europeischen Staatskunde. Butzow und Weimar, 1779, gr. 8vo. II Th. Die neueste mit Veränderungen bereicherte Auflage ist Butzow, Schwerin, und Weimar, 1785, gr. 8vo. II Th.

Voyages faits en 1771 & 1772 en diverses parties de l'Europe, de l'Afrique, & de l'Amerique, pour verifier l'utilité de plusieurs methodes, & instrumens servant a determiner la latitude, & la longitude, suivis de recherches pour rectifier les cartes hydrauliques,

drauliques, par M. M. Verdun, de Borda, & de Pingré. A Paris, 1778, 4to.

Voyages dans les cours de l'Europe. A Londres, 1752, 8vo. III vol.

Voyages en divers pays de l'Europe en 1774, 1776. A la Haye, 1777, 8vo. II tom. A Bâle, 1779, gr. 8vo.

WOLSKI (THOM. STAN.) peregrinatio Hierofolymitana latius producta per tres infigniores mundi partes, Europam, Afiam, & Africam. Leopoli, 1737, 1748, 4to.

WRAXALL, vide COPENHAGEN.

FERRO ISLANDS.

DEBES (LUC. JAM.) a defcription of the iflands and inhabitants of Ferro. London, 1676, 16mo.

DEBES (LUCAS JACOBSEN) Färeä referata. Copenh. 8vo.

----- Natürliche und politifche hiftorie der Infeln Faro; aus dem Danifchen, nebft Thormod Torfaeus Faroefche Gefchichte aus dem Lateinifchen überfetzt. Copenhagen und Leipzig, 1757, 8vo.

JONGE (NIC.) Chorographifk befkrivelfe Konigeriget Norge, famt Färoe iflands, och Grönland. Kiobenh, 1778, 4to.

KERGUELEN TREMAREC (DE) Relation d'un voyage

voyage aux côtes d'Iflande, de Gronlande, de Ferro, de Schettland, des Orcades, & de Norwege fait en 1767 & 1768. A Paris, 1771, 4to. Do. A Amfterdam, 1772, 4to.

The fame tranflated into German. Leipzig, 1772, gr. 8vo. *mit einem Kupfer und* 2 *Landcharten.*

FERNEY.

SHERLOCK, *vide* BERLIN.

FICHTELBERG.

BRUSCHII (CASP') Befchreibung des Fichtelbergs. Wittenberg, 1612, 4to. Vermehrt durch Theobaldus. Nurnberg, 1683, 4to.

PACHELBEL VON GEHOG (JOH. CHRISTIAN) Ausführliche Befchreibung des Fichtelbergs in Nordgau liegend. Leipzig, 1716, 4to.

WILLNS (J.) Deutfches Paradies, im vortrefflichen Fichtelberge, deffen Strömen, Bergwerken, Nutzbarkeiten, und Seltenheiten. Frankf. fol.

FIN.

FINLAND.

BLEFKENIUS (DITH,) Hiftorie von Lap—&
Finland, Hier is by gevoegt de Befchryving van Is—en Groenland. Leuwarden
1716, 8vo.

BURJA (ABEL) vide COURLAND.

HERMANNIDAE (RUTGERI) Deliciae five
amoenitates Sueciae, Gothiae, magnique
Ducatus Finlandiae. Lugd. Bat. 1705,
12mo.

HERMAN'S (BENED. FRANZ) Beyträge zur Phy-
fick, Oeconomie, Minerologie, Chymie,
Technologie, und Statiftick, befonders
der Ruffifchen und angrenzenden Ländern. Berlin, und Stettin, 1786, gr. 8vo,
1ter Band.

OWEXIONII (MICH) epitome defcriptionis Sueciae, Gothiae, Finningiae, & fubjectarum
provinciarum. Aboae, 1650, 8vo.

RUDBECK, vide ALAND,

ZEILLERI (M.) defcriptio regnorum Sueciae,
Gothiae, magnique Ducatus Finlandiae;
ut et Livoniae, Bremenfis Ducatus, Po-
meraniae. Amft. 1655, 12mo.

▪ ▪ ▪ ▪ ▪ ▪ ▪ ▪ Befchreibung des Königreichs
Schweden und Gothen, auch des Grofs-
fürftenthums

fürſtthenthums Finland, &c. Ulm, 1647, 8vo.

FLANDERS.

Beobachtungen auf einer Reiſe nach Paris durch Flandern, 1776. Leipzig, 1778, 8vo.

BURNEY, *vide* BOHEMIA.

CALVETE, *vide* BRABANT.

COULON (LOUIS) Voyage de France, de Flandres & de Savoye. 'A Paris, 1643, 8vo.

DESCHAMPS, *vide* BRABANT.

FRANK's (THOM.) Tour through France, Flanders and Germany. London, 1735, 8vo.

Le Guide de Flandres & de Hollande. 'A Paris, 1779, 8vo.

Lettres gallantes & de voyage, dans lesquelles on decrit les moeurs, les coûtumes, & les interêts d'Italie, d'Hongrie, d'Allemagne, de Suiſſe, d'Hollande, de Flandres, d'Eſpagne & d'Angleterre. 'A Paris, 1671, 12mo.

MARSHALL, *vide* DENMARK

Memoires & plans geographiques des principales places de France, d'Italie, d'Allemagne, d'Hollande

Hollande, & Flandre Efpagnole. A Paris, 1698, 8vo.

R. (DE LA) Voyage d'un amateur des arts en Flandres, dans les Païs Bas, en Hollande, en France, en Savoye, en Italie, en Suiffe, fait dans les années, 1775 jufqu' en 1778, dans lequel on indique les edifices, & les monumens antiques, & modernes, les collections de peinture, de fculpture, d' hiftoire naturelle, les bibliotheques, &c. une defcription des vallées de glace de Faucigny & de Berne. A Amfterdam, & fe trouve à Liége, 1783, 12mo. IV. tom.

REGNARD *vide* DENMARK.

ST. MARTIN *vide* BRABANT.

SINGLADE *vide* CORSICA.

Viaggio di un uomo qualificato *vide* ENGLAND.

FOREZ.

DULAC, *vide* BEAUJOLOIS.

FORMENTERA.

CAMPBELL (COLIN) ancient and modern hiftory of the Balearic iflands, with their natural and geographical defcription, tranflated from the Spanifh, 1616. 8vo.

RRANCHE COMTEE.

POCOCKE, *vide* ARCHIPELAGO.
R. (COMTE GREGOIRE DE.) *vide* CHAMPAIGN,
ROMAIN JOLI (FR. JOS.) La Franche Comtée
  ancienne & moderne. A Paris, 1779, 12mo.

FRANCE.

A descriptive journey through the interior parts of Germany & France including Paris, with interesting and amusing anecdotes by a young English Peer. London, 1786, 8vo.

A new journey to France, with several diverting transactions. London, 1715, 8vo.

Almanach du voyageur dans Paris, & dans les lieux les plus remarquables du royaume, pour l'année 1786. A Paris, 1786, 16mo.

ANDREWS (JOHN) Letters to a young gentleman on his setting out for France. London, 1784, 8vo.

BARETTI, *vide* ENGLAND.

BELLI (FRANC) Offervazioni fatte nel viaggio fatto col Sigr. Giorgi Ambafciatore Veneto in olanda, e Francia. Venez. 1632, 4to.

BENJAMINIS

BENJAMINIS NAVARRENI ITINERARIUM, *vide* EUROPE.

BERNOULLI (JEAN) Lettres fur differens fujets ecrites pendant le cours d' un voyage par l' Allemagne, la Suiffe, la France meridionale, & l' Italie en 1777, 1779, 8vo. III vol.

BERNOULLI, *vide* AUSTRIA.

BERNOULLI'S ARCHIV. *vide* BELLUNO.

Befchreibung einer Reife aus Deutfchland &c. *vide* ENGLAND.

BJOERNSTAEHL *vide* CONSTANTINOPLE.

BIRKENS (SIGIMUND VON) Reifen des Marggraf Chriftian Ernft zu Brandenburg durch Deutfchland, nach Frankreich, Italien und die Niederlande. Bareuth, 1669, 4to. Do. 1676, 12mo.

BLAINVILLE, *vide* ARCHIPELAGO.

BLANC (L' ABBE LE) *vide* ENGLAND.

BOCCAGE (MAD. DE) *vide* Do.

BOYLE (ROBERT) Voyages & avantures en France, en Suiffe, & en Italie, traduits de l' Anglois. A Amfterdam, 1730, gr. 12mo, II vol.

The fame tranflated into German. Halberftad, 1735, II Th. Hamburg & Leipzig, 1744, 8vo. II Th.

BREVAL *vide* ALSACE.

BROWN'S (EDWARD) travels and adventures in

in France, Italy, Malta, &c. London, 1739, 8vo.

BRUN DES MARETTES DE MOLEON (LE) Voyages liturgiques de France, avec des decouvertes fur l' antiquité ecclefiaftique & payenne, A Paris, 1718, 8vo.

BURNET (GILBERTS) Account of what feemed moft remarkable in Switzerland, Italy, Germany, & France. Rotterdam, 1686, 12mo. Do. 1686, 8vo.

The fame tranflated into French, Rotterdam, 1687, 12mo.

The fame tranflated into German, III Edit. Leipzig, 1693. 12mo.

The fame into Dutch. Hoorn, 1726. 8vo.

BURNEY vide BOHEMIA.

CASTILLO (DN. LEON DE) Viaje del Rey Dn. Felipe 4to. a la frontera de Francia. Madrid, 1667, 4to.

COUDRAY (DU.) Anecdotes intereffantes & hiftoriques de l' Illuftre voyageur Jofeph IId. pendant fon fejour à Paris. A Paris, 1777, 8vo. Leipzig, 1777, 8vo. A Paris, 1778, 12mo,

The fame tranflated into German. Augfburg, 1777, 8vo.

---------- Voyage du Comte de Hagen (Roi de Suede) en Italie & en France. A Paris, 1784, 8vo.

COULON vide FLANDERS.

By

--------- Fidele conducteur pour le voyage de France. A Paris, 1654. 8vo.

--------- Rivieres de France, ou description geographique & hiftorique des cours & debordemens des rivieres de France, avec le denombrement des villes, ponts & paffages. 'A Paris, 1644, 8vo. II tom.

DENIS (L.) Conducteur Francois contenant les routes avec un detail hiftorique & topographique des endroits, ou elles paffent, & des notes curieufes fur les chaines des montagnes, qu'on rencontre. 'A Paris VII parts, avec cartes.

Defcription générale, & particuliere de la France, enrichie d' eftampes. A Paris, 1781, gr. fol. tom. I.

DES LORD's * * * 1te und 2te Reife nach Paris. Berlin, 1780, 1781, 8vo. II Theile.

DEVIZE, Voyage des Ambaffadeurs de Siam en France. A Lyon, 1686, 12mo.

DUVAL-PYRAU (ABBE) Journal & anecdotes intereffantes de Monf. le Comte de Falkenftein en France. A Paris, 1777. Frankf. & Leipz, 1777, 8vo.

The fame tranflated into German. Frankf. & Leip. 1777, 8vo.

EBERT, *vide* ENGLAND.
EISENBERG, *vide* Ditto
ELVERI, *vide* Ditto
ENS (CASP.) Deliciae Galliae. Coloniac, 1609, 8vo.

8vo. État des Cours, *vide* EUROPE.

ERPENIUS (THOMAS) de peregrinatione Gallica utiliter inftituenda, Lugd. Bat. 1631, 12mo. Juncta Jufti Lipfii epiftola de peregrinatione Italica, &c. Hamburg, 1721, 8vo.

FABRI's (JOH. ERN.) Sammlung von Stadt,— Land,—und Reife-Befchreibungen. Hall, 1786, 8vo. II Theile. Enthält auch eine Uberficht der Univerfitäten, Academien, und anderer litterarifchen Anftalten in Frankreich.

FERDINAND ALBRECHT, *vide* ENGLAND.

FEVRE (LE) Journal hiftorique du voyage de l'Ambaffadeur de Perfe en France. 'A Paris, 1715, 8vo.

FORCE (PIGANIOL DE LA) Nouveau voyage de France. 'A Paris, 1755, gr. 12mo. II tom.

------ Nouvelle defcription de la France, dans laquelle on voit le gouverment général de ce royaume. 'A Paris, 1754, gr. 12mo. VIII tom.

FRANKS, *vide* FLANDERS.

GEISLER's (ADAM FRID.) Kaifer Jofeph's des IIten. unter den Namen eines Grafen von Falkenftein unternommene 2te. und 3te. Reife nach Rufsland, Niederland, und Frankreich. Hall, 1781, 8vo.

GERBERT (AB. MART.) Iter Allemannicum; accedit

cedit Italicum & Gallicum de anno 1760.
St. Blaſii, 1765, 1773; 8vo.
The ſame tranſlated into German. Ulm, Frankf. & Leipzig, 1767, 8vo.

GIRAUD SOULAVIE, Chronologie phyſique des eruptions des Volcans êteints de la France meridionale. A Paris, 1781, gr. 8vo.
The ſame, vide AUVERGNE.

GOELNIZII (ALB.) Ulyſſes Belgico—Gallicus, Lugd. 1631, 12mo, Amſterdam, 1655, 12mo.

GRASSERI SCHATZKAMMER, *vide* ENGLAND.
GRIMM *vide* Do.
GUALANDRIS, *vide* Do.
GUINDERODA *vide* Do.
H. (COMTE F. DE) *vide* Do.
HARTIG (GRAF VON) *vide* Do.
HEMPEL's (E. F.) Reiſender Deutſcher in Deutſchland, Italien, Frankreich, Niederland. Eine Wochenſchrift. Halle 1745, 1748, 8vo. IV Th.
HENTZNER *vide* ENGLAND.
HILL *vel* MARSHALL's travels through France and Spain, London, 1773. 8vo.
Tranſlated into German. Dantzig, 1778, 8vo.
Hiſtorical extracts relative to laws, cuſtoms, manners, trade, literature, arts, ſciences, &c. of France; tranſlated from the new
hiſtory

hiftory of Velly and others. London, 1769, 8vo. II vol.

HORNN, *vide* ENGLAND,

HUNCZOWSKY *vide* ALSACE,

JORDAN *vide* ENGLAND.

JOSTEN's (JACOB) Reifebefchreibung durch die Turkey, Ungarn, Pohlen, Preuffen, Böhmen, Oefterreich, Deutfchland, Spanien, Frankreich &c. Lubeck, 1652, 4to.

Journal einer Reife durch Frankreich, von der Verfafferin von Rofalien's Briefen, Altenburg, 1787, 8vo.

L. (C. F. H.) Reifebemerkungen, *vide* ENGDAND.

Le voyage de France dreffé pour l' inftruction & la commodité des êtrangers. A Rouen, 1647, 12mo.

LEMHARD (J.) Journal du voyage d' Anne Marie, Reine d' Efpagne, depuis Neubourg par la France jufqu' à Madrid. A Bruxelles, 1691, 8vo.

LIMBERG *vel* RODEN, *vide* ENGLAND.

LUTZENKIRCHEN (GUIL.) Deliciae apodemicae per Galliam & Hifpaniam. Coloniae 1609, 8vo.

M. Voyages faits en divers tems en Efpagne, Portugal, Allemagne, & France. A Amfterdam, 1690, 1700, 12mo.

M Reflections on D. Gilbert Burnet's travels into Switzerland, Italy, and certain

parts

parts of Germany and France. London, 1688, 8vo.

M. (T.) Reife der Päbſte nach Frankreich, Deutfchland, und Italien, 1782, 8vo.

MARSHALL, vide DENMARK.

MARCELL'S (C.) Reifen und Bemerkungen durch Frankreich, Italien und die Niederlande, aus dem Franzöſiſchen. Berlin und Potzdam, 1787, 8vo. IV Theil.

MARTENE (EDW.) & DURAND (URSIN) BENEDICTINS DE LA CONGREGATION DE ST. MAUR. Voyage litteraire en France, dans les Païs Bas, &, dans l'Allemagne, ou l' on trouve, 1ment, quantité de pieces, d' infcriptions, & d' epitaphes fervant à eclaircir l' hiſtoire, & les genealogies des anciennes familles. 2ment pluſieurs uſages des eglifes cathedrales & des monaſteres touchant la difcipline, & l' hiſtoire des Eglifes des Gaules; 3ment. les fondations de monaſteres & une infinité de recherches curieuſes & intereſſantes, qu'ils ont faits dans prés de 100 evechés & 800 abbayes, qu'ils ont parcouru. A Paris, 1717, 1724, gr. 4to. II vol.

N. B. This Book might be of great utility to fuch families as may have pretenfions or a right to claim inheritances of their anceſtors in France, the Low Countries or Germany.

MATHEWS voyage en France, *vide* ARCHIPE-LAGO.

MADRISIO (NIC.) Viaggj per l' Italia, Francia, e Germania, 1717, 8vo. II tom.

MAYER, *vide* BOHEMIA.

Memoires & plans geographiques, *vide* FLANDERS.

MERCKERII (JO.) apodemica, in itinere potiſſimum Gallico nata, & curforie confignata. Erfurt, 1634, 12mo.

MONT (DU) Voyage en France, en Italie, en Allemagne & en Turquie, contenant les recherches & obfervations curieufes, qu'il a faites en tous ces païs tant fur les moeurs, les coûtumes des peuples, & les differentes religions, que fur l' hiftoire ancienne & moderne, la philofophie, & les monumens antiques. A la Haye, 1699, 1700, gr. 12mo. IV vol.

MOORE's (JOHN) view of the fociety and manners in France, Switzerland and Germany. London, 1779, 1780, 8vo. II vol.

The fame tranflated into German. Leipzig, 1779, 8vo. II Bände.

MURALT, *vide*, ENGLAND.

NAVAGERO (ANDR.) Viaggio in Spagna ed in Francia nei anni 1524, 1528. In Venezia, 1563, 8vo.

NEUMAYER VON RAMSLA *vide* ENGLAND.

Nouvel itineraire general, *vide* Do.

Nouveau

Nouveau voyage de France, avec un itineraire. A Paris, 1724, gr. 12mo. II tom. avec 14 cartes.

Nouveau voyage de France geographique, hiflorique, & curieux. A Paris, 1738, gr. 12mo.

ORDER *vide* ENGLAND.

ORTELII (ABRAH.) & VIVIANT (Jö.) itinerárium per nonnullas Galliae & Belgii partes. Antw. 1584, 8vo. Lugd. Bat. 1660, 1667, 12mo.

The fame, vide BRABANT.

PALMER's four months tour through France. London, 1776, 12mo. II vol.

PILATI, *vide* EUROPE.

PONTANI (ISAAC) itinerarium Galliae Narbonnenfis cum duplici apendice & gloffario prifco—Gallico, feu de lingua Gallorum veteri differtatione. Lugduni, 1606, 12mo.

POOLE's (R.) journey from London to France, and Holland. London, 1742, 8vo.

POULLIN DE LUMINA moeurs & coûtumes des François. A Lyon 1768, 12mo. II tom.

QUADI (MAT.) Deliciae Galliae. Francof. 1603, 4to.

R. (DE LA) *vide* FLANDERS.

R. Lettres critiques & politiques fur les colonies & le commerce des villes maritimes de France adreffées à (G. Th.) Raynal. A Geneve & Paris, 1785, 8vo.

R. (M. L.) Nouveau voyage en France geographique

phique, hiftorique, & curieux. A Paris, 1723, 8vo.

Ray's (John) travels through the Low countries, Germany, Italy and France, with an account of the travels of Willoughby through Spain. London, 1738, 8vo. II vol.

--- -------- Iter per Belgium, Germaniam, Italiam, & Galliam. Londini, 1763, 8vo.

Rechac. Evenement du voyage du Prince Zara Chrift d' Ethiopie. A Paris, 1635, 4to.

Reifbefchryvinge door Vrankryk, &c. vide England.

Relation d'un voyage nouvellement fait par la France. A Londres, 1717, 8vo.

Remarks on the character and manners of the French. London, 1770, 8vo. II vol.

Roche (de la) journal ei: er Reife durch Frankreich. Altenburg, 1787, 8vo.

Roden, vide England

Rouviere (Henry de) Tour de la France. A Paris, 1712, 12mo.

Rutilii (Claudii) itinerarium, lib. II. Francof, 1623, 8vo. Amfterd. 1687, 8vo. Altenb. 1741, 8vo. Brandenburgi 1760, 8vo.

S. Voyage de France, d' Efpagne, de Portugal, et d' Italie. A Paris, 1770, IV tom.

Sagittarii (Thom) vide England.

Salzmann's (Fried. Rud.) Brieftafche auf einer Reife durch Deutfchland, Frankreich, Helvetien

Helvetien und Italien. Frankfurt, 1780. 8vo.

SANDER's (HEINR.) Befchreibung feiner Reifen durch Frankreich, Niederland, Holland, Deutfchland, und Italien. In Beziehung auf Menfchenkenntnifs, Induftrie, Litteratur, und Naturkunde infonderheit. Leipzig, 1783, 8vo. II Theile.

SAVINIEN D' ALQUIE (FR.) Delices de la France. Amfterdam, 1670, 12mo. II vol.

SCHAMBERGII (SIMON) deliciae Galliae. Francof, 1616, 24to.

SCHEID, vide ENGLAND.

SCHONDORFER (JOH. HIERON) Hofmeifter nach Frankreich, oder Anweifung, was die Deutfchen in Frankreich fehen und lernen können. Nurnberg, 1673, 12mo.

SCHOTTI (FRANC.) itinerarium Italiae, Germaniaeque; accedit ejufdem itinerarium Galliae & Hifpaniae. Colon, 1620, 12mo.

SINGLADE, vide CORSICA.

SMOLLET's (J.) travels through France and Italy. London, 1766, 8vo. II vol.

The fame tranflated into German, Leipz. 1767, 8vo. II. Theil.

Sommaire defcription de la France, de l' Allemagne, de l'Italie, et de l'Efpagne. A Cologne, 1605, 12mo.

STERNE's (L.) Sentimental journies through France and Italy. London, 1768, 1770,

12mo

12mo II vol. Leipzig, 1771, 8vo. II vol.
Altenb. 1776, 8vo. II vol. Göttingen, 1779,
8vo. II. vol.

The fame tranflated into German. Hamburg und Bremen, 1768, 1769, 8vo. II Th.

The fame tranflated into French. A Paris. 1769, 12mo. II tom.

Reifen durch Frankreich und Italien, als ein Verfuch über die menfchliche Natur. Braunfchweig, 1769, 8vo.

STEVEN's (SCHAVERELL) vermifchte Anmerkungen, einer neulich gethanen fieben-jährigen Reife durch Frankreich, Italien, Deutfchland, und Holland. Aus dem Englifchen. Gotha, 1759, 8vo.

STORCH's (H.) Skizzen, Scenen, und Bemerkungen auf einer Reife durch Frankreich. Heidelberg, 1787, gr. 8vo.

STROBELBERGER (Jo. STEPH.) Galliae politico-medica defcriptio, de qualitatibus regni Gallici, academiis, urbibus, fluviis, aquis medicatis, acre, plantis, mineralibus differens. Jenae, 1621, 12mo.

TEMPLE's (LANCEL) Short ramble through fome parts of France and Italy. London, 1771, 12mo.

The tour of Holland, vide BRABANT.

THICKNESSE, vide CATALONIA.

THOMPSON's (CHARLES) travels, containing his obfervations on France. London, 1748, 8vo. 3 vols.

VER-

VERDIER (DU) Voyage de France dreffé pour l'inftruction tant des François, que des étrangers, A Paris, 1639, 1685, gr. 12mo.

VERDUN, *vide* DENMARK.

VERYARD's (E.) account of choice remarks in a journey through the Low Countries, France, Italy, part of Spain, Sicily and Malta; as alfo to the Levant. London, 1701, fol.

Viaggio d'un uomo qualificato, *vide* ENGLAND.

VOLKMANN's (D. T. T.) neuefte Reifen durch Frankreich in Abficht auf Naturgefchicht, Oeconomie, Manufacturen, und Werke der Kunft, &c. Leipzig, 1787, 8vo. 1ter Band.

Voyage pittorefque de la France, avec la defcription de toutes les provinces. A Paris, 1784, 1785, gr. fo. XXXI livraifons.

WELSCHEN. *vide* ARCHIPELAGO.

WRAXALL (NATH.) Tournées dans les provinces occidentales, meridionales, & interieures de la France, trad. de l' Anglois. A Rotterdam. 1777, 12mo.

WRIGHT's (EDWARD) Some obfervations made in travelling through France, Italy, &c. in the years 1720, 1721, 1722. London. 1730, 4to. II vol. in Blainville's travels.

YORICK's empfindfame Reifen 3ter & 4ter Theil. Hamburg, 1769, 8vo.

Q   ZEITTRS

ZEILLER's (M.) itinerarium Galliae.
ZINZERLINGII (JUSTI) SUB NOMINE SINCERI itinerarium Galliae. Amsterdam, 1656, 12mo.

FRANCONIA.

ANDROPHILI Beschreibung vieler Städté in Franken, Sachsen, und Schlesien: Hamburg & Breslau, 1735, 8vo.
BERNOULLI, vide AUSTRIA.
GERCKEN, vide BAVARIA.
GERCKENS Forst setzung, vide Do.
Tagebuch eines Hofmeisters vide Do.

FRIULI.

BROWN's (EDW-) vide AUSTRIA.
POCOOKE vide ARCHIPELAGO.

GENEVA.

M*** Voyage de Geneve & de la Tourraine. A Orleans, 1779, 12mo.
SAUSSURE vide ALPS.
SHERLOCK (M.) vide BERLIN.

GENOA

GENOA.

BARETTI, *vide* ENGLAND,
HEYSL (HANS) Philip IIten Königs von Spanien Reife aus Spanien nach Genua, Italien, Deutfchland, &c. von 1549, bis 1551 Augfburg 1571, 4to.

GERMANY.

A DESCRIPTIVE JOURNEY, *vide* FRANCE.
APELBLAD (JON.) Ströda Anmerkingar famlar under en Refa igenom Tyfka Orter. Stockholm, 1778, 8vo.
ASHLEY's (JON) Briefe, aus dem Englifchen überfetzt. Bern, 1782, 8vo.
AUSTEL's (HENRY) Voyage to Ragufa, and thence to Conftantinople, Moldavia, Polonia, Silefia, and Germany. In Hackluyt's principal navigations, *vide* ANGLESEY.
BARDILI (JOH. WEND) Reifen Maximilian Emanuel's Printzen von Wurtemberg durch Deutfchland, &c. Stutgard, 1739, 8vo. Do. Frankf. und Leipzig, 1739, 8vo.
BAUMANN's (P. C.) Benutzte Reife durch Deutfchland und Welfchland, &c. nebft einem

einem Land—und Haußwirthſchaftlichen Kalender- Augſburg 1782, 8vo.

BEAUJEU (DE) Memoires contenant ſes voyages en Pologne, en Allemagne, & en Hongrie, A Paris 1698, 12mo. A Amſterdam 1700, 12mo.

Bemerkungen über einige Gegenden des Catholiſchen Deutſchlands. auf einer kleinen gelehrten Reiſe gemacht. Nurnberg, 1777, 8vo.

BENJAMINIS NAVARRENI ITINERARIUM, vide EUROPE.

BERNOULLI (T.) vide FRANCE.

The ſame vide BELLUNO.

BERNOULLI'S SAMMLUNG 13ter UND 14ter BAND, vide AUSTRIA.

BEYRLIN (JACOB) Reiſe durch Deutſchland, Pohlen, Spanien &c. 1604, 4to.

BJOERNSTAEHL, vide CONSTANTINOPLE.

BIRKEN vide FRANCE.

BLAINVILLE, vide ARCHIPELAGO.

BOETTICHER (JOH. GOTTL.) Bemerkungen auf einer Reiſe durch Deutſchland. Hall, 1778, 8vo.

BREVAL, vide ALSACE.

BROWN, vide AUSTRIA.

BRUCE (PETER HENRY) Memoirs containing an account of his travels in Germany, Ruſſia, Tartary, &c. London, 1772, gr. 8vo.

The

The same translated into German. Leipzig, 1784, gr. 8vo.

BRUIKMANN (FRANC. ERN.) Epistolae itinerariae. Wolfenbut. 1750, 1753, 4to.

BURNET (GILBERT) *vide* FRANCE.

BURNEY, *vide* BOHEMIA.

CASINI DE THURY, *vide* AUSTRIA.

CHAPPUZEAU, Allemagne protestante, ou relation d'un voyage aux cours des Electeurs, & des Princes protestans de l' Empire en 1669, &c. A Geneve, 1671. 4to.

COSTA (MARGHERITA) Storia del viaggio d' Allemagna del Gran Duca di Toscana, Ferdinando II. In Venezia, 4to.

COULON (L.) Fidele conducteur pour le voyage d' Allemagne. A Paris, 1654, 8vo.

D.*** Voyage historique & politique de Suisse, d' Italie, & d' Allemagne. A Frankf. 1736, 1737, 1743, gr. 12mo. III tom.

DENINA, *vide* BRANDENBURGH.

Der neugierige Passagier auf Reisen in Deutschland, und den Niederlanden. Frankf. & Leipzig, 1767, 4to.

EBERT (ADAM) *vide* ENGLAND.

EICHOFII (CYPR.) Deliciaarum Germaniae index. Ursellis, 4to.

ELVERI deliciae apodemicae, *vide* ENGLAND.

FERDINAND ALBRECHT, *vide* Do.

FISCHERS

FISCHER's hydrographie von Deutſchland, in Fabri's Sammlung, *vide* FRANCE.

FRANKS, *vide* FLANDERS.

GERBERT, *vide* FRANCE.

GRIM, *vide* ENGLAND.

HANWAY's (JON) hiſtorical account of the Britiſh trade in the Caſpian Sea, with a journal of his travels from London through Ruſſia, into Perſia, and back again through Ruſſia, Germany and Holland. London, 1753, 4to. II vol. Do. Dublin, 1754. 8vo. II vol.

The ſame tranſlated into German. Hamburg & Leipzig, 1754, gr. 4to. *II Theil. Leipzig,* 1769, gr. 4to. *II Th.*

HEBERER VON BRETTEN, *vide* DENMARK.

HEMPEL, *vide* FRANCE.

HENZNER, *vide* ENGLAND.

HERVEY's (CHR.) Letters from Spain, Italy and Germany, in the year 1759, 1761. London, 1785, 8vo. III vol

HEYSL, *vide* GENOA.

HOLLENBERG's Bemerkungen über verſchiedene Gegenſtände auf einer Reiſe durch einige Deutſche Provintzen, vornehmlich in Anſehung der Architectur, Mechanic, &c. Stendal, 1782, 8vo.

HOPFERI (BENED.) ſtricturae ad iter Germanicum Dan Eremitae. Tub. 1688, 12mo.

JOR's

JARS VOYAGES METALLURGIQUES *vide* ENGLAND.

JOSTEN, *vide* FRANCE.

Judicium de Sinceri Germanici itinerario politico, 1669, 12mo.

KEYSSLER, *vide* BOHEMIA.

KINDLEBEN, *vide* DRESDEN.

KINDLINGER'S (VENANT) Munsteriche Beyträge zur Geschichte Deutschlands, hauptsächlich Westphalens. Munster, 1787, 8vo.

KUSELII (SALOMON) itinerarium Germaniae, Italiae, Siciliae, vicinarumque insularum peregrinationes continens, Erphord, 1617, 8vo.

L. (DE) Voyage en Allemagne et en Pologne commencé en 1776. A Amsterdam, 1784, 12mo.

LAPIDE (SINCERI GERM. A) Mercurius Germanicus, seu itinerarium Germaniae politicum, modernam principuarum aularum Imperii faciem repraesentans. Cosmopoli, 12mo.

LEDYARD'S (THOMAS) German Spy, or familiar letters from a gentleman on his travels through Lower Germany, &c. London, 1740, 8vo

The same translated into English. Lemgo, 1764, 8vo.

Lettres curieuses de voyage, *vide* ENGLAND.
Lettres galantes & de voyage, *vide*, FLANDERS.
LIMBERG VEL RODEN, *vide* ENGLAND.
Litterarische Reise durch Deutschland. Leipzig, 1786, 8vo. I Band.
LUC (J. A. DE) Lettres physiques & morales addressées à la Reine de la Grande Bretagne sur l'histoire de la terre et des hommes. A la Haye, & à Paris, 1779, 8vo. V tom.
The same translated into German by Gehler. Leipzig, 1781, 1782, gr. 8vo. II Th.
LYNAR's (G) Reisen durch Ober Deutschland, Westphalen, &c. in Bernoulli's Sammlung, *vide* AUSTRIA.
M. Reflexions on D. Burnet's travels, *vide* FRANCE.
M. * * * * voyage de Geneve, *vide* GENEVA.
M. (C. P. D.) relation, *vide* ENGLAND.
M. (T.) Reise der Päbste, *vide* FRANCE.
MABILLONII (Jo.) iter Germanicum, Hamburg, 1717, 8vo.
MADRISIO, *vide* FRANCE.
MARSHALL, *vide* DENMARK.
MARTENE & DURANT, *vide* FRANCE.
MAYER, *vide* COURLAND.
Memoires & plans, *vide* FLANDERS.
MONCONYS, *vide* CONSTANTINOPLE.

MONT,

MONT, *vide* FRANCE.

MONTAGNE (MICH. DE) Journal du voyage en Italie, en Suiffe, & en Allemagne, avec des notes par Monfr. de Querlon. A Paris, 1774, gr. 4to. A Berlin, 1774, 8vo. II tom. A Rome, 1775, 12mo. III vol.

The fame translated into German. Hall, 1777, 8vo. II. Th.

MOORE *vide* FRANCE.

Neue Reifebemerkungen, *vide* BERLIN.

NICOLAI (FRID) Befchreibung einer Reife durch Deutfchland, und die Schweitz im Jahr 1781, nebft Bemerkungen uber die Gelehrfamkeit, Induftrie, Religion, und Sitten. Berlin, 1783, gr. 8vo. II. Th. 1784, 3ter. und 4ter. Th. 1785, 1786. 5te. 6te. und 7te. 1787, 8te. Th.

NUGENT'S (THO.) travels through Germany, with a particular account of the Court of Mecklenburg. London, 1768. 8vo. II vol.

The fame tranflated into German, with remarks. Berlin, 1781, 1782, gr. 8vo. II Th.

PATIN, *vide* BOHEMIA.

PAYEN, *vide* BRABANT.

PENN'S (WILL.) account of travels in Holland and Germany, in the year 1675. London, 1695, 8vo.

PILATI *vide* EUROPE.

R   Po-

Pocockе, *vide* Archipelago.
Potamographia, *vide* Europe.
Puel's (Martin) Reifen und Seefahrten von Steyer durch Deutfchland, Ungarn, Italien, &c. Nurnberg, 1666, 4to.
Quadi (Math.) Deliciae Germaniae. Colon. 1600. 4to.
Ratgeben und Schickhard, *vide* Denmark.
Ray, *vide* France.
Regnard *vide* Denmark.
Reifebefchryvinge door Vrankryk, *vide* England.
Reifen und Begebenheiten, *vide* England.
Remarques d'un voyageur fur la Hollande, l'Allemagne, l'Italie, l'Efpagne, le Portugal. A la Haye, 1728, 8vo. Do. 12mo.
Remarques hiftoriques, *vide* Austria.
Richard (P. F.) Briefe eines aufmerkfamen Reifenden durch Deutfchland die Mufic betreffend. Frankf. & Leipz. 1774, 1776, 12mo. II Th.
Riesbeck (Casp) Brieffe eines reifenden Franzofen durch Deutfchland an feinen Bruder in Paris, aus den Französischen überfetzt, 1783, gr. 8vo. II Th.
River's (Lord) Briefe von und an denfelben während feines zweyten Aufenthalts in Deutfchland aus deffen original Papieren überfetzt. Leipzig, 1782, 8vo.

Ro-

RODEN, *vide* ENGLAND.
ROHAN (DUC DE) *vide* Do.
ROSMITAL and BLATNA, *vide* Do.
SALTZMANN, *vide* FRANCE.
SAGITTARII ULYSSES SAXONICUS *vide* ENGLAND.
SANDER *vide* FRANCE.
SCHWEIGGER *vide* CONSTANTINOPLE.
SCOTTI ITINERARIUM *vide* FRANCE.
SEIDEL *vide* CONSTANTINOPLE.
SHERLOCK, *vide* BERLIN.
SINGLADE *vide* CORSICA,
Sommaire description *vide* FRANCE.
SOMMER *vide* ARCHIPELAGO.
STEVEN- SCHAVERELL, *vide* FRANCE.
SULZER, *vide* EUROPE.
Taschenbuch für Reisende durch die vornehmsten Städte von Europa, besonders Deutschland nebst verschiedenen andern Nachrichten. Berlin, 1781, 8vo.
TITIUS Reise durch Deutschland in Bernoulli's Sammlung, *vide* AUSTRIA.
ULRICH (JOH. HEINR. FRID.) Bemerkungen eines Reisenden durch die Preusischen Staaten. Altenburg, 1779, 1781, 8vo. III Th.
Viatorium Germaniae, Galliae, & Italiae. Frankfurt, 1671, 12mo.
VITALE (FRANC. ANT.) epistola ad Ferdin.

Elepantitium

Elepantitium de fuo in Germaniam itinere. Florent, 1780.

Voyage hiftorique de la Suiffe, d' Italie, & d' Allemagne, Frankf. 1736, II tom.

Voyages faits en divers tems en Efpagne, Portugal, Allemagne, France, &c. Amfterdam, 1699, 8vo.

WECKHERLIN UNTER DEN NAHMEN RABIOSUS *vide* AUSTRIA.

WELSCHEN *vide* ARCHIPELAGO.

WILLEBRAND (JOH. PET.) Nachrichten von einer Carlfbader Brunnen Reife, von J. H. K. Leipz. 1780, 8vo.

ZEILLER's (MART.) Reifebuch durch Hoch und Nieder Deutfchland. Strafburg, 1765, fol.

---------- Reifegefehrte durch Ober und Nieder Deütfchland. Nurnberg, 1786, 12mo.

GIBRALTAR.

CARTER (FRANCIS) Journey from Gibraltar to Malaga, &c. London, 1777, 8vo. II vol.

The fame in German, Leipzig, 1779, 8vo. *II Theil.*

JAMES's (THOMAS) Hiftory of the Herculean ftraits. London, 1771, 4to.

Kurtze doch zuverläffige Befchreibung der Infel

fel Minorca, des Forts St Philip, und der Feftung Gibraltar. Leipzig, 1782, 8vo.

VOLCKARD'S REISEN, *vide* AMSTERDAM.

Zufätze zu der Befchreibung der Feftung Gibraltar. Leipzig, 1783, 8vo.

GLARIS.

AFSPRUNG (JOH. MICH.) Reife durch einige Cantone der Eidgenoffenfchaft, nemlich von Ulm nach St. Gallen, Appenzell, Glaris, Ury, Schweitz, Zug, und Zurch. Leipzig, 1734. 8vo.

PFENDLER'S (HEINR.) Gründliche Befchreibung der hohen Berge, Fruchtbarkeit, wilden Thieren, Natur, und andern Wunderdingen des Landes Glaris. Bafel, 1670, 12mo.

GLOUCESTERSHIRE.

ATKIN'S (ROBERT) The ancient and prefent ftate of Gloucefterfhire. London, 1768, fol. II vol.

RUDDER's new hiftory of Gloucefterfhire, comprifing the topography, antiquities, curiofities, trade and manufactures. Gloucefter, 1778, fol.

GLOCK-

GLOCKNER Mountain in Tyrol.

Hacquet (B.) *vide* Carniola.

GOTHA.

Wili, *vide* Altorff.
Neue Reisebemerkungen, *vide* Berlin.
Tagebuch einer Reise von der Westphälischen Gräntze uber Arolsen, Cassel, Gotha, und Weimar nach Leipzig. Leipzig, 1786, 8vo.

GOTHLAND.

Hermannidae deliciae Sueciae *vide* Finland.
Kalm (Pehr.) Wästgöta och Bahuslandska resa. Stockholm, 1746, 8vo.
Linnaei (Carl.) Olanska, och Gothlänska resa. Stockholm, 1745, 8vo.
Malgo's voyage, in Hackluyt's principal navigations, *vide* Anglesey.
Owexionii (Mich) epitome *vide* Finland.
Praetorii (Matth.) Orbis Gothicus, seu historia de originibus, sedibus, linguis, regimine, Regibus, moribus, & conversione

ad

ad fidem omnium Gothici orbis populorum.
Libri IV. Olivae, 1688, fol.

ZEILLER, *vide* FINLAND.

St. GOTTHARD (MOUNT.)

PINI (HERMENEGILD) mineralogifche Beobachtungen uber das Gebürg des St. Gotthard; aus den Italienifchen uberfetzt von Beyer. Schneeberg, 1784, 8vo.

GREECE.

BELONS (DU MANNS) PIERRE, Obfervations de plufieures fingularités, & chofes memorables trouvées en Greece, Afie, &c, A Paris, 1588, 4to.

The fame in Latin. *Antw.*1589. 8vo.

BENJAMINIS NAVARRENI ITINERARIUM *vide* EUROPE.

BJOERNSTAEHL, *vide* CONSTANTINOPLE.

CASTEL *vide* Do.

CHANDLER'S (RICHARD) travels into Greece. Oxford & London, 1776.

- - - - - - - - *tranflated into German. Leipzig*, 1777, *gr.* 8vo.

- - - - - - - *into Dutch. Utrecht*, 1779, *gr.* 8vo.

CHOISEUL-GOUFFIER (COMTE DE) Voyage pittorefque

toresque de la Grece. A Paris, 1779, 1780
11 cahiers.

The same translated into German, by Reichard.
Gotha, 1780, 1782, 8vo 1ter. 2ter. Heft.

CONSTANTIN THE GREAT, EMPEROUR AND
KING OF BRITAIN, Voyage to Greece in
Hackluyt's principal navigations, *vide*
ANGLESEY.

DOUSAE (GEORG) *vide* CONSTANTINOPLE.

GILLIES (J.) Geschichte von Alt Griechenland, und deffen Pflanzstädten, uud Eroberungen, aus den Englischen. Leipzig, 1787, 8vo. 1 Th.

GUILLET, Lettres ecrites sur la differtation d'un voyage de la Grece, publiées par Mr. Spon. A Paris, 1679, 12mo.

GUYS, Voyage litteraire de la Grece. &c. A Paris, 1771, gr. 12mo. II tom. Augmenté A Paris, 1776, gr. 8vo. II vol. Do. 1783, gr. 4to II tom.

The first edition translated into German. Leipzig, 1772, 8vo. *II Th.*

GUY's Briefe über die neuen Griechen—in den kleinen Reifen, *vide* COLOGNE.

Journey through Italy, Greece, and Egypt, from a French officer.

LUCAS (PAUL) Second voyage l'an 1704, 1708, dans la Grece, &c. A Paris, 1710, 12mo. II vol. A Amsterdam, 1714, 8vo. II tom.

The same translated into German. Hamburg, 1715, 8vo.

M. (C. D. S.) Nouveau voyage de la Grece, *vide* ALSACE.

MIRABEL, Voyage d'Italie, & de la Grece. A Paris, 1698, 8vo.

MOTRAYE, *vide* CRIM.

PALERNE, *vide* ARCHIPELAGO.

PAUSANIAE Graeciae descriptio, Graece & Latine, cum Amasei verſione. Florent. 1551, fol. Hanov. 1613, fol. Lipſiae, 1696, fol.

The same translated from the Greek into French, by Gedoyn, with remarks. A Paris, 1781, *4to. II tom. Do. A Amsterdam,* 1733 *8vo. II tom. avec cartes,*

Do. from the Greek into German, with observations by Goldhagen. Berlin & Leipzig, 1766, *8vo, II Th. & 1 Karte.*

PERRY, *vide* CONSTANTINOPLE.

PIACENZA, *vide* ARCHIPELAGO.

POCOCKE, *vide* Do.

SANDY'S (JORG) travels into Turkey, &c. begun in the year 1610. London, 1632, fol. Do. 1658, fol.

The same translated into Dutch. Amsterdam, 1654, 4to.

Do. into German, Frankf. 1669, 12mo.

SPON & WHEELER *vide* DALMATIA.

Spon (Jacques) Reponse à la critique publiée par Mr. Guillet, sur le voyage de la Grece. A Lyon, 1679, 12mo.

Sprengel, *vide* England.

Struys (Jan Jansen) Gedenkwaerdige Reisen door Italie, Griekenland, Livland, Moscovien, Tartarye, &c. Amsterdam, 1667, 4to.

The same translated into German, by Muller. Amsterdam, 1678, fol.

Do. into French. Amsterdam, 1720, 12mo. III vol.

Sulivan (R. J.) *vide* Europe.,

Voyage Historique de la Grece. Amsterdam, 1733, 8vo. IV tom.

Wheeler's Journey, *vide* Dalmatia.

GREENLAND.

Anderson (Joh) Efterretningen om Island, Gronland, og strat Davis, &c. Kiobenh. 1748, 8vo.

------ Nachricht von Island, Groenland, und der Straße Davis. Frankf. & Leipz. 1747, 8vo.

The same translated into French. A Paris, 1754, 8vo. II tom.

------ Natural History of Iceland, &c. 1758, fol.

Blef-

BLEFKENII (DITHMAR) Iflandia, &c. cum quibusdam de Groenlandia adjectis. Lugd. Bat. 1607, 4to.

The fame tranflated into Dutch. Groeninghen, 1780, 8vo.

BLEFKENIUS, vide FINLAND.

CRANTZ (DAVID) Hiftorie von Groenland. Barby, 1765. 1770, 8vo.

The fame tranflated into Englifh from the High Dutch. London, 1767, 8vo. II vol.

DALAGER (LARS) Groenlandfke relationer. Copenh. 1758, 4to.

DOES (JORIS VAN DER) verfcheyde voyagien, vide CONSTANTINOPLE.

EGEDE (HANS) det Gamle Groenlands nye perluftration. Ciopenh. 1720, 1741, 4to.

The fame translated into German, Copenh. 1742, & Berlin, 1763, 8vo.

Do. into Englifh. London, 1745, 8vo.

Do. into Dutch. Delft, 1746, 4to.

Do. into French, A Copenh. &. a Geneve, 1763, 8vo.

FABRICIUS (DAN) De Iflandia & Groenlandia. Roftoch, 1616, 1vo.

H. (A. G.) Befchreibung des Groenlandifchen Wallfifchfangs, und Urfachen des Nordlichts, mit Anmerkungen herausgegeben von Tramplar. Leipzig 1781,

1781, 8vo.

Hiſtoriſche Nachricht von den Drangſalen des 1777 auf den Wallfiſchfang nach Groenland abgefahrnen verunglückten Schiffes Wilhelmina. Bremen, 1779, 8vo. aus dem Holländiſchen überſetzt.

JONGE, *vide* FERRO ISLANDS.

JONSOEN (JONAE) Groenlandia, Kiob. 1732, 8vo.

KERGUELEN, *vide* FERRO ISLANDS.

MARTEN's (FRID) Spitzbergiſche und Groenlandiſche Reiſebeſchreibung von 1671. Hamburg, 1675, 4to.

The ſame translated into Engliſh, London, 1694, 4to.

------ Viaggio alla Spitzberga, e Greenlanda. In Bologna, 1680, 12mo.

MARTINIERE (DE LA). Nouveau voyage des pays Septentrionaux l'année 1653, 12mo. Do. A Amſterdam, 1708, 12mo.

The ſame translated into German. Hamburg, 1675. 4to. Glückſtad, 1675, 4to. Do. mit annehmlichen Nordlichen Curioſitäten vermehrt von Herring. Leipzig, 1703, 1711. Ditto, 1718, 8vo.

MESANGE (PIERRE DE) La vie, les avantures, & le voyage de Gronlande, avec une relation de l'origine, de l'hiſtoire, des moeurs, & du du paradis des habitans du pole arctique. A Amsterdam, 1720, gr. 12mo. II tom.

MUNK (JAN.) Beskrivelle af Seigland. og resa til Nova Dania. Ciopenh. 1619.

PEYRERE (ISAAC DE LA) Relation de Gronlande. A Paris, 1715, 8vo.

The same translated into German, by Silvers Hamburg, 1764, 4to.

PURCHAS (SAM.) Pilgrims, &c. London, 1726, fol.

STAUNING kort beskrivelse över Grönland. Viborg 1775, 8vo.

THORLACIUS, Letter concerning the ancient state of Iceland and Greenland, in Hackluyt's principal navigations:*vide* ANGLESEY.

TORFAEI (THOREN) Gronlandia antiqua Hafniae, 1706, 1708, 1715, 8vo.

Udtog af Breve fra de Kongens, soe Officerer der ere beordrede til af oplede gamle Gronland. Kiob. 1786, 8vo.

Y. (S. VON) Neueste Beschreibung des alten und neuen Grönlands nebst einem Begriff der Reisen die Forbisser, Gotze, Lindemann, Reichard, &c. nach Norden gethan; mit Anführung des Tagebuchs eines die Durchfahrt zwischen Groenland und America suchenden Dänischen Schiffs. Hamburg, 1674, Nurnberg, 1679, 4to.

WOLF (JAN. LAUR.) Norriges, Islands, og
Greenlands

Greenlands Beſkrivelſe. Ciopenh. 1651, 4to.

ZORGDRAGER (CORN. GISBERT) Groenlanſche viſchery en de walviſchfangſt. II edit. Delft, 1646, 4to,

The ſame tranſlated into German. Nurnberg, 1750, 4to.

Do. into Engliſh. London, 1725, *under the title "View of the Greenland trade and Whale fiſhery, with the national and private advantages thereof.*

GRISONS, COUNTRY OF THE.

SPRECHERI (FRID.) Rhaetia, Lugd. Bat. 1633, 24mo.

TSCHUDI (ÆGID.) DeſcriptioRhaetiaeAlpinae. Baſil, 1538, 4to.

GUERNSEY.

Hiſtoire detaillée des iſles de Jerſey, & Guernſey, traduite par le Rouge. A Paris, 1757, 12mo.

HAGUE.

SHERLOCK, *vide* BERLIN.

HAMBURG.

AUBERY DE MAURIER, *vide* DENMARK.
BURNEY, *vide* BOHEMIA.
Neue Reisebemerkungen, *vide* BERLIN.
VOLCKARD, *vide* AMSTERDAM.

HANOVER.

Neue Reisbemerkungen, *vide* BERLIN.
Relation der Reise Königs Georg des Iten von Hanover nach London. Hamburg, 1714, 8vo.

HERTFORDSHIRE.

Sketch of a tour, *vide* BEDFORDSHIRE.

HARWICH.

DALE's natural history of the Sea coast and country about Harwich. London, 1730, 4to.

TAYLOR's

TAYLOR's (THOM.) natural hiftory of the fea-
coaft and country about Harwich. London
1730, 4to.

H A R Z.

BEHREN's (GEORG HENNING) Hercynia cu-
riofa. Nordhaufen, 1703, 4to.
BERNOULLI *vide* AUSTRIA.
GATTERER's (Ch. W.I.) Anleitung den Harz
und andere Bergwerke mit Nutzen zube-
reifen. Gottingen, 1785, 1786, 8vo. II Th.
GÖTZE (T. A. E.) Kleine Harzreifen. Leipzig,
1785, 1786, 8vo.
Neue Reifebemerkungen, *vide* BERLIN.
ROHR (JUL. BERN VON) Merkwürdigkeiten des
Vor—und Unter Harzes. Frankf. 1756,
8vo.
- - - - - - - - - Merkwürdigkeiten des Oberharzes. Faankf. 1739, 8vo.
SCHROEDER (CHRIST. FRID.) Abhandlung
von Brocken, und den ubrigen Alpini-
fchen Gebürgen des Harzes. 1ter Th. Deffau, 8vo.
ZIMMERMANN's (EBR, AUG. WITH) Beobachtungen auf einer Hartzreife, nebft einem
Verfuch die Höhe des Brockens durch
den Barometer zu beftimmen. Braunfchweig, 1775, 8vo.

ZUCKERT

ZUCKERT's (JOH. FRID) Natur gefchichte und Bergwerksverfaſſung des Oberharzes. Berlin. 1762, 8vo.

---------- Naturgefchichte einiger Provintzen des Unterharzes, nebſt einem Anhang von den Mansfeldifchen Kupferfchiefern. Berlin, 1763, 8vo.

HEBRIDES.

ANDERSON's (JAMES) Account of the prefent ſtate of the Hebrides and Weſtern coaſts of Scotland. London, 1786, 8vo.

BOSWELL's (JAMES) Journal of a tour to the Hebrides with Johnfon. London, 1785, 8vo.

Translated into German. Lubeck, 1787, 8vo.

JOHNSON's (SAM.) Journey of the Weſtern Iflands of Scotland. London, 1775, 8vo.

The fame translated into German. Leipz. 1775, 8vo.

MAC NICOL's (DNALD) Remarks on Johnfon's Journey, London, 1780, 8vo.

MARTIN's (M.) Late voyage to St. Kilda, the remoteſt of all the Hebrides. London, 1698, 8vo.

------- Defcription of the Weſtern iflands of Scotland. London, 1704, 1716, 8vo.

PENNANT's (THOM.) tour in Scotland, and voyage to the Hebrides. London and Chester, 1774, 1776, 4to. II tom. 44. C.
The same translated into German. Leipzig, 1779. 1780, 8vo. II Th.

HERMANSTADT.

LAHMAN's (Jos) Reise von Presburg nach Hermannstadt in Siebenburgen. Dunkelspiel und Leipzig, 1785. 8vo.

HERRNHUT.

Briefe über Herrnhut, und andere Örter der Oberlausnitz. Winterthur, 1787, 8vo.

HESSE.

APELBLAD (JONES) Beschrifning ofwer Saxen. Stockholm, 1759, 8vo.
The same translated into German. Berlin und Leipzig, 1785, 8vo.
RASPE (RUD. ERICH) Beyträge zur allerältesten und natürlichen Historie von Hesser. Cassel, 1774, 8vo.

--- Ac-

------- Account of the German volcanos (in Hesse) and their productions. London, 1776, 8vo.
VALENTINI (MICH. BERN.) prodromus historiae naturalis Hassiae. Giess. 1707, 4to.
WINKELMANN's (JOH. AUG.) gründliche Beschreibung der Fürstenthümer Hessen und Hersfeld. Bremen, 1711, fol.
WOLFARTH (PET.) naturalis historiae Hassiae pars 1ma. Cassel, 1719, fol. & 25 Ch.
Reise durch das Hessische Gebiet und angrenzende Länder. Freystadt, 1780, 8vo.

HOLLAND.

A trip to Holland. London, 1786. 12mo. II vol.
BEAUMARCHAIS (A. DE LA BARRE DE) Le Hollandois, ou lettres sur la Hollande ancienne & moderne. A Frankf. 1738, gr. 8vo. II part.
BELLI, vide FRANCE.
BERKLEY (LE FRANCH VAN) Natuurlyke historie van Holland. Amsterdam, 1769, 1774, gr. 8vo. III deelen.
The same translated into German; Leipz. 1779, 1782, *II Bände.*

BERNOULLI, *vide* AUSTRIA.
-------- 13ter & 14ter Band, *vide* Do.
-------- ARCHIV. *vide* BELLUNO.
Befchreibung einer Reife, *vide* ENGLAND.
BJOERNSTAEHL, *vide* CONSTANTINOPLE.
BLAINVILLE, *vide* ARCHIPELAGO.
BOCCAGE, *vide* ENGLAND.
COYER (ABBE) Voyages d' Italie & de Hollande. A Paris, 1769, 12mo. II tom. & 1775, 8vo. II tom.
Tranflated into German. Nurnberg, 1776, 8vo.
Defcription of Holland and the United Provinces. London, 1743, 8vo.
EBERT, *vide* ENGLAND.
FEBURE (BARON DE ST. ILDEPHONT GUILLE) Itineraire hiftorique, politique, geographique des VII provinces unies des Païs Bas, A la Haye, 1782, 12mo. II tom-
GRIM, *vide* ENGLAND.
GUINDERODA, *vide* Do.
HANWEY, *vide* GERMANY.
HEGENITII (GOTHOF) Itinerarium Frifio— Hollandicum. Lugd. Bat. 1767, 12mo.
JORDAN, *vide* ENGLAND.
Kleine Reifen, *vide* ERMENONVILLE.
Le Guide de Flandres & de Hollande, *vide* FLANDERS.
Le voyageur bienfaifant, ou anecdotes du voyage de Jofeph II. dans les Païs Bas,

la

la Hollande, &c. A Liege, 1781, 8vo. & a Paris, 1781.

Les delices de la Hollande. A la Haye, 1706, 1710.

Lettres Hollandoifes. A Amfterdam, 1747, 1750, 8vo. II tom.

Lettres galantes, *vide* ENGLAND.

LOMENII, *vide* AUSTRIA.

M. (C. P. D.) *vide* BOHEMIA.

MARCILLY (GUILLOT DE) Relation hiftorique & theologique d'un voyage en Hollande, &c. A Paris, 1719.

MARSHALL, *vide* DENMARK.

Nieuwe geographifche, Nederlandfche Reife en zee—atlas, mitfgaders eene beknoopte algemeene geographie dezer provintzen. t'Amfterdam, 1773, 8vo.

OEDER, *vide* ENGLAND.

PATIN, *vide* BOHEMIA.

PAYEN, *vide* BRABANT.

PENN, *vide* GERMANY.

PERTELII (FRID. WILH.) commentarii de republica Batava. Lugd. Batav. 1782, 8vo.

— — — — — — — *Tranflated into German.* Berlin, 1784, 8vo.

PILATI (CHARLES ANT. DE) Lettres fur la Hollande ecrites, 1778, 1779. A la Haye, 1780, 12mo. II tom.

Trans-

Tranſlated into German. Berlin and Stettin, 1782. II Th. 8vo.

POOLE, vide FRANCE.
RT. (DE LA) vide FLANDERS.
REGNARD, vide DENMARK.
Reiſe-Beſchryvinge, vide ENGLAND.
Relation du voyage de Sa Majeſté Brittannique Guillaume III en Hollande. A la Haye. 1692, fol.
Relation of the voyage and reſidence which King Charles II. made in Holland, 1660, fol.
Remarques d'un voyageur ſur la Hollande, vide GERMANY.
SANDER, vide FRANCE.
SAVINIEN d'ALQUIE (FR.) Delices de la Hollande. Amſterdam, 1669, 12mo.
SCHEID, vide ENGLAND.
SPOERT's (JOH. CONR. CHR.) vermiſchte Briefe, welche zum Theil Reiſe-beſchreibungen auch Nachrichten von Holland, Surinam, Spanien, Algier, &c. enthalten. Langenſalza, 1786, 8vo. Iter. Th.
SPRENGEL vide ENGLAND.
STEVEN vide FRANCE.
The tour of Holland, vide BRABANT.
UFFENBACH, vide ENGLAND.
VIAGGIO DI UN UOMO QUALIFICATO, vide ENGLAND.

VOGEL's

VOGEL's (JOH. WILH) Journal seiner Reise nach Holland, und Ost-Indien. Leipz. 1690, 1696, 12mo.

HOLSTEIN.

AUBERY DE MAURIER, *vide* DENMARK.
BUCHWALD (FR. VON) Udtog af en Reisendes Dag---Bog i Mecklenborg, Pommern, og Hollsteen. Kiob. 1784, 8vo.
The same translated into German. Copenh. 1786, 8vo.
HERMANNIDAE, *vide* DENMARK.
HOLK, *vide* DENMARK.
Neue Reisbemerkungen, *vide* BERLIN.
ZEILLER, *vide* DENMARK.

HUNGARY.

BEAUJEU, *vide* GERMANY.
BERNOULLI, *vide* AUSTRIA.
BORN (IGNATZ VON) Briefe über mineralogische Gegenstände auf einer Reise durch den Temeswarer Banna', Siebenbürgen, Ober und Nieder Ungarn. Frankf. & Leipzig, 1774, 8vo.
BROWN, *vide* AUSTRIA.
BRUICKMANN, *vide* GERMANY.

CHROSNEL's

CHROMER's (MARTIN) mitternächtlicher Völker Historie. Basil 1562, fol.

EDELINGII hodocporicon vide AUSTRIA.

EDMUND AND EDWARD IN HACKLUYT's PRINCIPAL NAVIGATIONS, vide ANGLESEY..

FERBER's (JOH. IAC) physikalisch-metallurgische Abhandlungen über die Gebürge und Bergwerke in Ungarn. Nebst einer Beschreibung des Steirischen Schmelzens, und Stahlmachens. Berlin und Stettin, 1780, 8vo.

HAPPELI (EBERH. GUER) thesaurus exoticorum, nebst einer Beschreibung von Ungarn. Hamburg, 1688, fol.

JOSTEN, vide AUSTRIA.

KEYSSLER, vide BOHEMIA.

LABOUREUR, vide GERMANY.

LETTRES galantes, vide ENGLAND.

LETTRES. curieuses, vide Do.

POCOCKE, vide ARCHIPELAGO,

POSSEVINI (ANT.) Moscovia & alia opera, Praeterea Werner de admirandis Hungariae aquis. Colon. 1595, fol.

PUEL, vide GERMANY.

RATHGEBEN und SCHICKHARD, vide DENMARK.

SEIDEL, vide CONSTANTINOPLE.

SOMMERS, vide ARCHIPELAGO.

SULZER, vide ALSACE.

TOLLII epistolae, vide BERLIN.

WALLSDORFF's (CHR. VON) Reifebefchreibung durch Ungarn, Thracien, &c.
WILDEN, vide CONSTANTINOPLE.
ZEILLER's (M.) Befchreibung des Königreichs Ungarn, vermehrt durch Beza. Leipzig, 1690, 8vo.

I C Y   S E A.

Allgemeine Hiftorie der Reifen, vide CANARY ISLANDS.
MULLER's (J. F.) voyages from Afia to America, for compleating the difcoveries of the North-weft of America, to which is prefixed a fummary of the voyages of the Ruffians on the frozen fea. London, 1761, 1764, 4to.
-------- Voyages & decouvertes faites par les Ruffes le long des côtes de la mer glaciale & fur l' ocean, &c. A Amfterdam, 1766, 8vo. II tom.

I C E L A N D.

ANDERSON, vide GREENLAND.
Avertiffement om Anderfon's Traƒtat om Ifland, Kiob. 1748, 8vo.
BLEFKENII Iflandia, vide GREENLAND.
BLEFKENIUS vide FINLAND.

DOES (JORYS VAN DER) *vide* CONSTANTI-
NOPLE.

EGGERHARD (OLAV.) Enarrationes hiſtoricae
de Iſlandiae natura & conſtitutione. Hafniae, 1749, 8vo.

EGGERS (CHR. ULR. DETLEV) phyſicaliſche
und ſtatiſtiſche Beſchreibung von Iſland,
aus authentiſchen Quellen, und nach den
neueſten Nachrichten. Kopenh, 1786, I
Theil.

FABRICIUS, *vide* GREENLAND.

HACKLUYT *vide* ANGLESEY.

HORREBOW (NILS) tilforladeliga efterretnin-
ge om Iſland. Kiopenh. 1750, 8vo.

The ſame tranſlated into German. Leipzig, 1683.

KERGUELEN TREMAREC, *vide* FERRO-ISLANDS.

Letters from Iceland containing obſervations on
the civil, litteral, eccleſiaſtical and natural
hiſtory, antiquities, volcanos, baſaltes, hot
ſprings, cuſtoms, dreſs and manners of the
inhabitants; made by Banks, Solander,
Lind, Troil, &c. London. 1780, 8vo.

MARTINIERE, *vide* GREENLAND.

MOHR (N.) Forſög til en Iſlandſk natur hiſtorie
med adſkillige oeconomiſke ſamt andere
anmerkinger. Kiob. 1786, 8vo.

OLAFFEN'S OG POVELSEN'S reiſe igienem
Iſland, &c. Sorve, 1724, 4to. II deele.

--------- Reiſe durch Iſland veranſtaltet
von

von der Königl. Societät der Wiffenfchaften in Copenhagen, gethan von 1752 bis 1757. Copenh. und Leipz. 1774, 1775, 4to. II Theil.

OLAVIUS (E.) Ockonomifk reife igienem de Nordweftlige, Nordlige, og Nordoftlige kamter af Ifland. Kiobenh. 1783, 4to. *Tranflated into German. Drefden & Leipzig,* 1787, gr. 4to.

PEYRERE (ISAAC DE) relation de l' Iflande. A Paris, 1663, 8vo. A Amfterdam, 1715. Philofophifche Schilderung der gegenwärtigen Verfaffung von Ifland, nebft Stephenfon's Befchreibung des Erdbrands im Jahr, 1783, &c. Altona & Leipzig, 1786, 8vo.

RAMUSIO (GIO. BATT) raccolte di navigazioni, e viaggi. In Venez, 1613, fol. III tom.

STRAUCH (ÆGIDIUS) De Iflandia. Witteb. 1670, 4to.

TORKELSON'S (JON., tilgift til Anderfon om Ifland. Kiobenh. 1748, 8vo.

THORLACII (THEOD.) differtatio chorographico-hiftorica de Iflandia. Viteb. 1661, 4to

TROIL (UNO) Bref rörende en refa til Ifland, 1772. Upfal, 1777, 8vo. *The fame tranflated into German. Upfala & Leipzig,* 1779,

ZORGDRAGER *vide* GREENLAND.

IRELAND

IRELAND.

A tour through Ireland in feveral entertaining letters. London, 1748, gr. 8vo.

A Philofophical furvey of the South of Ireland, in a feries of letters to John Watkinfon. London, 1777, 8vo.

The fame tranflated into German. Breflau, 1779, 8vo.

B. (R.) admirable curiofities *vide* ENGLAND.

BARTON's (RICH) dialogue concerning points of importance in Ireland.

BEEVERELL *vide* ENGLAND.

BERKENHOUT *vide* Do.

BOATE's (GERH) Ireland's natural hiftory, London, 1652, 8vo. Dublin, 1753, 4to. III part.

The fame tranflated into French. A Paris. 1666, 12mo.

BUSH's (JOHN) Hibernia curiofa. London, 1764, 8vo.

CAVE (THOM) De origine, moribus, ritibufque gentis Hibernicae. Sulzbach, 1666, 4to.

HAMILTON, *vide* ANTRIM.

HACKLUYT, *vide* ANGLESEY.

HARTLIEB's (SAM.) Ireland's natural hiftory. London, 1652, 8vo.

HERMANNIDAE, *vide* ENGLAND.

KUETTNER'S (CARL GOTTFR) Briefe über Irland. Leipzig, 1785, 8vo.

MISSON, *vide* ENGLAND.

PETTY'S (WILL) political survey of Ireland. London, 1719, 8vo.

RUTTY'S (JOHN) essay towards a natural history of Ireland. Dublin, 1722, gr. 8vo. II vol.

Sammlung der besten und neuesten Reisebeschreibungen *vide* ENGLAND.

IOVII descriptio Brittanniae, *vide* ENGLAND.

TWISS (RICH) tour in Ireland, 1775. London, 1776, 8vo.

The same translated into German. Leipzig, 1777, 8vo.

VOLKMANN'S (JO. JAC.) neueste Reisen durch Schottland, und Irland, vorzüglich in Absicht auf die Naturgeschicht, Oeconomie, Manufakturen, und Landsitze der Groſſen. Leipzig, 1784, gr. 8vo.

YOUNG'S (ARTHUR) tour in Ireland. London, 1780, 8vo. II vol,

The same translated into German, Leipzig, 1780, 8vo. II *Th.*

ZEILLER *vide* ENGLAND.

ISTRIA

I S T R I A.

HACQUET, *vide* CARNIOLA.
POCOCKE, *vide* ARCHIPELAGO.

I T A L Y.

ADDISON's (JOSEPH) remarks on feveral parts of Italy. London, 1736, 12mo.
ALBERTI (LEANDRO) defcrizione di tutta l' Italia. In Bologna, 1550 4to. In Venez. 1581, 4to.
ALDON, *vide* EUROPE.
AMBROSII (ABBATIS CAMALDULENSIS) hodoeporicon, feu defcriptio itineris juffu Eugenii Papae per Italiam, 1431, fufcepti. Flor. 1678, 4to. Luccae, 1681, 4to.
ARCHENHOLZ, *vide* ENGLAND.
AUDEBERT (GERMAIN) Voyage d'Italie. A Paris, 1656, 8vo.
BARBARO (ANT. TOMASO) Pellegrino da Napoli fino a Venezia. In Venezia, 1738, 12mo.
BARETTI (JOS) Account of the manners and cuftoms of Italy. London, 1768, 1769, 8vo. II vol.
  The fame tranflated into German. Breflau, 1781, 8vo. II Th.
---------- Les Italiens. A Paris, 1774, 12mo.

BARRI (GIAC) Viaggio pittoresco d' Italia. In Venezia, 1671, 12mo.

BAUMANN, *vide* GERMANY.

BENJAMINIS NAVARRENI itinerarium, *vide* EUROPE.

BERNOULLI, *vide* AUSTRIA.

-------- Lettres sur differens sujets, *vide* FRANCE.

-------- Zufätze zu den neuesten Reisbeschreibungen von Italien. Leipzig, 1777, 1778, 1782, gr. 8vo. III Bände.

BJOERNSTAEHL, *vide* CONSTANTINOPLE.

BIRKEN *vide* FRANCE.

BLAINVILLE, *vide* ARCHIPELAGO.

BOCCAGE, *vide* ENGLAND.

BOYLE, *vide* FRANCE.

BREVAL, *vide* ALSACE.

BROME's (JAM.) travels through Portugal, Spain, Italy, &c. London, 1712, 8vo.

BROWN, *vide* FRANCE.

BULIFON (ANT.) journal du voyage d'Italie de Philippe V. A Naples, 1704, 8vo.

BURDE (SAM. GOTTL.) Erzählung von einer gesellschaftlichen Reise durch einen Theil der Schweitz, und des Obern Italiens, 1779 und 1780. Breslau, 1785, 8vo.

BURNET, *vide* FRANCE.

BURNEY, *vide* BOHEMIA.

CELLIUS, *vide* ENGLAND.

CITRILES, Merkwürdige Begebenheiten auf feiner 12 jährigen Reife durch Italien. Frankf. & Leipzig, 1782, 4to.

COCHIN voyage d'Italie. A Laufanne, 1773, 8vo. III tom.

CORKE AND ORERY (JOHN EARL OF) Letters from Italy, in the years 1754, 1755. London, 1773, 8vo.

The fame tranflated into German. Leipzig, 1775, 8vo.

COUDRAY, vide FRANCE.

COYER vide HOLLAND.

Curiofe und vollftändige Reifebefchreibung von gantz Italien. Freyburg, 1701, 4to.

D. * * * voyage hiftorique. vide GERMANY.

Defcrizione iftorica, e critica dell' Italia, o nuove memorie fullo ftato attuale del governo, delle fcienze, delle arti, del commercio, della popolazione, e della ftoria naturale. Londra, 1781, III vol.

Deliciae Italiae. Lipfiae, 1599, 12mo. Francof. 1609. 12mo.

Defcriptio Italiae brevis & accurata. Ultraj. 1650, 12mo.

EBERT, vide ENGLAND.

ENS (CASP) Deliciae Italiae. Colon. 1609, 8vo.

ERPENIUS, vide FRANCE.

FABRIS (JO. BAPT DE) Itinerarium philofophicum. Venet. 1632, 4to.

FERBER's

FERBER's (JOH. JAC) Briefe aus Welfchland uber die naturliche Merkwurdigkeiten diefes Landes. Prag, 1773, gr. 8vo.
The fame tranflated into Englifh. London, 1776, 8vo.
Do. into French. A Strafbourg, 1776, gr. 8vo.
FERDINAND (ALBRECHT) vide ENGLAND.
FERMANEL, voyage d'Italie & du Levant. A Rouen, 1587, 8vo.
FICORONI (FRANC. DE) Offervazioni fopra l' antichità di Roma. In Roma, 1709, 4to.
GERBERT, vide FRANCE.
GRASSERI (Jo. JAC) itinerarium hiftorico-politicum. Bafil, 1624, 8vo.
GROSLEY, Nouveaux memoires, ou obfervations fur l'Italie, & fur les Italiens par deux gentilfhommes Suedois. A Londres, 1764, gr. 12mo. III tom.
The fame tranflated into German. Leipzig, 1766, III Th. 8vo.
Do. into Englifh. London, 1769, II vol.
Guide pour le voyageur d'Italie, avec la notice de toutes les poftes & leurs prix. A Florence, 1779, 8vo.
HACKLUYT, vide ANGLESEY.
HAMILTON's (WILH.) neuere Beobachtungen uber die Vulcane Italiens, und am Rhein; nebft merkwürdigen Bemerkungen des

X   Abts

Abts Giraud Soulavie; aus dem Französischen. Frankf. & Leipzig, 1784, 8vo.

HARTIG, *vide* ENGLAND.
HEMPEL, *vide* FRANCE.
H. (COMTE F. DE) *vide* ENGLAND.
HENZNER, *vide* ENGLAND.
HERMANN, *vide* AUSTRIA.
HERVEY, *vide* GERMANY.
HEYSL, *vide* GENOA.
HOENN, *vide* ENGLAND.
HUGUETAN, Voyage d'Italie, augmenté par Spon. A Lyon, 1681 12mo.
HUYSSEN's (HENRIK VAN) Teegenwoordige toeftand van het Paufelike Hoff, &c. Utrecht, 1696.
JAGEMANN's (CH. JOS) Briefeuber Italien. Weimar, 1778, 1789, 8vo. *II Bande.* 1785 *IIIter Band.*
Journey through Italy, *vide* GREECE.
KEYSSLER's, *vide* BOHEMIA.
KLAUTE's (JOH, BATH) diarium Italicum. Caffel, 1722. fol.
Kleine Reifen, *vide* ERMENONVILLE.
KUSELII itinerarium, *vide* GERMANY.
L. (C. F. H.) *vide* ENGLAND.
LABAT (J. B.) Voyage en Efpagne & en Italie. A Amfterdam, 1731, 8vo. VIII tom.
The fame tranflated into German. Frankf. & Leipz. 1758, 1761, 8vo. VIII Th.

LABORDE (DE) Voyage pittoresque d'Italie &
de Sicile. A Paris, 1779, 1781, fol. tom
III.

LAMBERG, vide CORSICA.

LANDE (DE LA) Voyages d'un François en Italie.
A Yverdun, 1769, 1770, 12mo. VIII tom.

LASSEL (RICHARD) Voyage d' Italie traduit
de l'Anglois. A Paris, 1682, gr. 12mo. II
vol.

-------- *Translated into German by Salbach,
Frankf*, 1696, 12mo.

Les delices d'Italie contenant une defcription
du païs, &c. A Paris, 1707, 4tom.

Le veritable guide des voyageurs en Italie;
François & Italien. A Rome, 1775,
12mo.

Lettres curieufes de voyage *vide* ENGLAND.

LIMBERG vel RODEN, *vide* ENGLAND.

LOMENII itinerarium, *vide* AUSTRIA.

M. reflections on Burnet, *vide* FRANCE.

M. Lettres ecrites de Suiffe, d' Italie, de Sicile, et de Malthe. A Paris, 1780, 12mo.
VI vol.

M, (C. D. S.) *vide* ALSACE.

M. (T) Reife der Päbfte, *vide* FRANCE.

MABILLONII & GERMAIN, Mufeum Italicum,
feu collectio veterum fcriptorum ex bibliothecis Italicis eruta. Lut. Par. 1687, 1689,
4to. II tom.

MADRISIO, *vide* FRANCE.

Manuel du voyageur en Italie. A Rome & à Paris, 1785, 16mo. II part.

Manuel de l' étranger, qui voyage en Italie. A Paris, 1778, 12mo.

MARCELL, *vide* FRANCE.

MATHAEI (CARD. ST. ANGELI, EPISCOPI GURCENCIS,) Odoeporicon, i. e. itinerarium in Italiam. Viennae, 1515, 4to.

MATHEWS, *vide* ARCHIPELAGO.

MAYER, *vide* BOHEMIA.

Memoires & plans, *vide* FLANDERS.

MENCII (BALTH) itinera VI a diverſis Saxoniae Ducibus & Electoribus, Alberto animoſo, Erneſto, Friderico III, Henrico bis, & Johanne Georgio I, in Italiam omnia, tria in Paleſtinam facta, Witteb. 1612, 8vo.

MILLER's (MRS.) letters from Italy deſcribing the manners. cuſtoms, antiquities, paintings of that country; in the years 1770, 1771. London, 1776, 8vo. III vol.

MIRABAL, *vide* GREECE.

MISSON (MAXIM) Nouveau voyage d' Italie fait en 1688. A la Haye, 1691, 12mo. II vol. A Utrecht, 1722, gr. 4to. IV tom.

The ſame tranſlated into German. Leipzig, 1713, 8vo, III Th.

De.

- Do. into English: London, 1714, 8vo. II vol.

Do into Dutch. Utrecht, 1724, 4to. II deelen.

MOLLERI (DAN. WILH) progressus de praeparatione itineris in Italiam. Aldorf, 1679, 4to.

MONCONYS, vide CONSTANTINOPLE.

MONTFAUCON (BERN. DE) diarium Italicum, seu monumentorum veterum, bibliothecarum, musacorum, &c. notitiae singulares. Parisiis, 1702, gr. 4to,

The same translated into English. London, 1725, fol.

MONT (DU) vide FRANCE.

MONTAGNE, vide GERMANY.

MOORE's (JOHN) view of the society and manners in Italy, &c. London, 1780, 8vo. II vol.

The same translated into German. Leipzig, 1781, 8vo.

The same into French. A Lausanne, 1784 12mo. II tom.

MOTRAYE, vide CRIM.

NEMEITZ (JACOB CHR.) Nachlese besonderer Nachrichten von Italien, als ein Supplement von Misson, Burnet, & Addison, Leipzig, 1726, 8vo. II Th.

NEUMAYR VON RAMSLA (JOH. WILH) Reise durch

durch Welfchland, und Hifpanien. Leipzig, 1612, 4to.

NODOT obfervations, qu' il a faites pendant fon voyage d' Italie fur les monumens de l'ancienne, & de la nouvelle Rome. A Amfterdam, 1706, 12mo. II tom.

NORTHAL's travels through Italy. London, 1766, 8vo.

Obfervations fur l' Italie. A Paris, 1774, 8vo. 4 vols.

ORLANDI (CESARE) Delle città d' Italia, e fue ifole adjacenti compendiofe notizie. In Perug. 1770, 4to. tom. I.

PAKENII (Jo.) Hercules prod, feu Carolus Iuliae, Cliviae, Montium Princeps, Italiam profectus, in Johanne Wilhelmo, Comite Palatino nepote poft faeculum Italiam itidem, 1674, 1676, proficifcente redivivus. Col. Agrlp. 1695, 4to.

Paradifus deliciarum Italiae. Wurtzburg, 1657, 12mo.

PAYEN, *vide* BRABANT.

PFLAUMERN (JOH. HEIN. A) Mercurius Italicus hofpiti fidus. Aug. Vind. 1625, 1650, 8vo.

PIGHII (STEPH. VINANDI) Hercules prod. feu principis juventutis Caroli Friderici, Principis Juliaci, Cliviae, &c. 1575, Romae mortui vita & peregrinatio in Italiam

Italiam. Antw. 1587, 8vo. Argent, 1609, 8vo.
PILATI, *vide* EUROPE.

PLATIERE (ROLAND DE LA) Lettres ecrites de Suiſſe, d' Italie, de Sicile, & de Malthe en 1776, 1778. A Amſterd. & Paris, 1782, gr. 12mo. VI tom.

The ſame tranſlated into German. Hamburg, 1785, 8vo. II Th.

POCOCKE, *vide* ARCHIPELAGO.
PUEL, *vide* GERMANY.
R. (DE LA) *vide* FLANDERS.

RABELAIS (F.) Lettres pendant ſon voyage d' Italie. A Bruxelles, 1710, 8vo.

RATHGEBEN ET SCHICKHARD, *vide* DENMARK,

RAY, *vide* FRANCE.

RAYMUND's (JOHN) itinerary through Italy in the years 1646, 1647. London, 1748, 12mo.

Reiſbeſchryvinge, *vide* ENGLAND.
Reiſen und Begebenheiten, *vide* ENGLAND.
Reiſen eines Officiers durch die Schweitz, und Italien, Hanover, 1786, 8vo.

Remarques d'un voyageur, *vide* GERMANY.
Remarques hiſtoriques, *vide* AUSTRIA.

RICCOBALDI (ROMUALDO) Apologia del diario Italico del padre Montfaucon contra le oſſervazioni di Ficcoroni. In Venez. 1710, 4to.

RICHARD

RICHARD (ABBE) Defcription hiftorique & critique d'Italie, &c. A Paris, 1769, 8vo. 6 tom.]

The fame tranflated into Italian. In Firenze, 1782, 8vo. *VI tom.*

RICHARDSON's account of fome of the ftatues, bas reliefs, drawings, and pictures in Italy. London, 1722, 8vo.

RIESCH (ISAAC WOLF BARON DE) Obfervations faites pendant un voyage en Italie. A Drefde, 1781, 8vo. II tom.

RODEN, *vide* ENGLAND.

ROGISSART (DE & H***) Delices de l' Italie. A Leide, 1706, 12mo. III tom. Do. 1726, 12mo. VI tom.

The fame tranflated into German. Berlin, 1706, 8vo. *III Th.*

ROHAN, *vide* ENGLAND.

ROSMITAL and BLATNA, *vide* Do.

RUTILII itinerarium, *vide* FRANCE.

S. ( ) *vide* Do.

S. (J. C.) Ausfuhrliche Reifebefchreibung durch Italien. Frankf. 1673, 12mo.

Sammlung der beften und neueften Reifebefchreibungen, *vide* CYPRUS.

SALTZMANN's Brieftafche, *vide* FRANCE.

SANDER, *vide* Do.

SANDYS, *vide* GREECE.

SCHIKARDS VON HERNBERG (HEINR) Befchreibung einer Reife Herzogs Frid. von Wurtemberg

Wurtenberg durch Italien. Tubingen, 1603, 4to.

SCHOTTI itinerarium, *vide* FRANCE.

SCOTO (ANDR.) nuova defcrizione di viaggi principali d' Italia. In Venez, 1615, 12mo. III part. In Roma, 1737, 8vo. III vol.

SEINE (FR. DE) nouveau voyage d' Italie. A Lyon, 1699, 12mo.

SHARP's letters from Italy defcribing the cuftoms and manners of that Country in 1765. London, 1768, 8vo.

SHERLOCK, *vide* BERLIN.

S. *vide* FRANCE.

SMOLLET, *vide* Do.

Sommaire defcription *vide* Do,

SPON, *vide* DALMATIA.

STERNE, *vide* FRANCE.

STEVEN, *vide* Do.

STRUYS, *vide* GREECE.

SULZER, *vide* EUROPE.

SYMEON (GABRIEL) illuftres obfervations antiques en fon voyage d' Italie l' an 1557. A Lyon 1558, 4to.

TEMPLE, *vide* FRANCE.

THOMPSON, *vide* Do.

TOLLI (JACOB) Infignia itinerarii Italici, quibus continentur antiquitates facrae. Trajecti ad Rhenum, 1696, 4to.

TORRES (ANT. DE.) Saggio di rifleffioni fulle arti ed il commercio Europeo di noftri tempi,

Y

tempi, e delli antichi per illuſtrare alcuni
paſſi dell' iſtoria filofofica e politica. In
Pefaro, 1781, 1782, 4to. II tom.

VERYARD, *vide* FRANCE.

Viaggio d' un uomo qualificato, *vide* ENGLAND

VILLAMONT (DE) Voyages en Italie & en Pa-
leſtine. A Paris, 1614. 8vo.

VOLKMANN'S (JOP. JAC.) hiſtorifchcritifche
Nachrichten von Italien, welche eine ge-
naue Reifebefchreibung diefes Landes, der
Sitten und Gebräüchen, der Regierungs
form, Handlung und Oeconomie, des Zu-
ſtandes der Wiſſenſchaften, und infonderheit der Werke der Kunſt enthalten.
Leipzig, 1778, gr. 8vo. III Th.

Voyage hiſtorique. *vide* GERMANY.

Voyage hiſtorique d' Italie contenant des recherches exactes fur le gouvernement, les
moeurs, les fêtes, les fpectacles, & les fingularités des villes. A la Haye, 1729, 12mo.
II vol.

------- Voyage du Prince de Condé en Italie en 1625. A Paris, 1666, 12mo.

WELSCHEN, *vide* ARCHIPELAGO.

WRIGHT, *vide* FRANCE.

YORIK, *vide* Do.

ZACHARIAE (FR. ANT.) excurſus litterarii per
Italiam ab anno 1742—1752. Venet. 1754, 4to.

Iter litterarium ab anno 1753—1757. Venet.
1762. 8to.

ZEILLER

ZEILIER (M.) itinerarium Italiae. Francof. 1640, fol.

JUTLAND.

HENNING's Oeconomifche und ftatiftifche Betrachtungen einer in Jahr 1779 unternommenen Reife durch Jutland. Kopenh. und Leipzig, 1786, 8vo.

KENT.

HASTED's (EDW.) hiftory and topographical furvey of the county of Kent. Canterb. 1778, fol.

LAMBARD's perambulation of Kent. London, 1596, 4to.

KERRY.

SMITH's natural & civil hiftory of the county of Kerry. Dublin, 1756. 8vo.

KIEL.

BERNOULLI's Sammlung in 10ten Band *vide* AUSTRIA.

KILDA, St.

MARTIN, vide HEBRIDES.

KILIA NOVA.

KLEEMANN vide ARCHIPELAGO.

KUPFERBERGHEN.

HUELPHER (ABR) Dagbök ofwer en Refa igenom de under Stora Kopperbergs hofdinge döme lydande Lähn och Dalerne Wäſterås 1762, ſtor. 8vo. med Landchart

LANCASHIRE.

LEIGH, vide CHESHIRE.

LANGUEDOC.

ASTRUC)JEAN) memoires pour l' hiſtoire naturelle du Languedoc. A Paris 1740, gr. 4to. III tom.

BERNOULLI im 12ten Band, vide AUSTRIA.

FAUJAS DE ST. FOND, Recherches fur les Volcans éteints du Vivarais, & du Velai en Languedoc

Languedoc, avec un discours sur les Volcans brulans. A Grenoble & à Paris, 1779, gr. fol.

GENSSANE (DE) histoire naturelle de Languedoc. A Montpellier, 1776, 8vo. II tom.

GIRAUD SOULAVIE, vide AUVERGNE.

Kleine Reisen, vide ERMENONVILLE.

LANDE (DE LA) Des canaux de navigation, & specialement du canal de Languedoc. A Paris, 1778, fol.

LAPLAND.

ANDERSON, vide GREENLAND.

BLEFKENIUS, vide FINLAND.

Bibliothek der neuesten Reisebeschreibungen in Auszügen. Frankf. und Leipzig, 1780, 1782, 8vo. V Bände.

BOEMI (Jo.) mores, leges, & ritus omnium gentium, 1604, 8vo.

HOGSTROEM (PETER) Beskrifning öfwer de til Swenska Krona lylande Lapmarkene. Stockholm, 1747, 8vo.
The same translated into Danish. Kiøbenh. 1748,
Do. in German, in Fabris Sammlung, vide FRANCE.

KALM (P.) De oeconomia & moribus incolarum Lapponiae Kimiensis. Aboae, 1754, 4to.

KEILG-

KLINGSTEDT (DE) Memoires sur les Samoiedes & les Lappons. A Konigsberg, 1762, 8vo. A Kopenh. 1766, 8vo.

LEEM (KNUD) Beskrivelse öfwer, Finmarkens Lapper. Kiobenh. 1767, 4to.

The same translated into German. Leipzig. 1767, 4to.

MARSHALL, vide DENMARK.

MARTINIERE, vide GREENLAND.

MOTRAYE, vide CRIM.

NEGRI (FRANC) Lapponia. In Venezia, 1705, 8vo.

OERN's (NIC.) Beschreibung Laplands. Bremen, 1707, 12mo.

OUTHIER, journal d'un voyage au Nord de Messrs. de Maupertuis, Camus, & Clairaut, en 1736 & 1737. A Amsterdam, 1745, 12mo.

REGNARD, vide DENMARK.

RUDBECK, vide ALAND.

SCHEFFERI (JOH.) Lapponia. Francof. 1678, 4to.

SCHILLER, vide BOTHNIA.

WILLOUGHBY's (HUGH) voyage to Lapland, in Hackluyt's navs. vide ANGLESEY.

LA-

L A V I S.

Schinz, *vide* Bellentz.

L A U S A N N E.

R. (Comte Gregoire de) *vide* Champaign.
Sherlock, *vide* Berlin.

L E I C E S T E R.

Burton's (Will.) defcription of Leicefter-
fhire. London 1622, 1777, fol.
Sketch of a tour into Derbyfhire, *vide* Bedfordshire.

L E M B E R G.

Boscowich (Jos.) journal d' un voyage de
Conftantinople en Pologne, en 1762. A
Laufanne 1722, 12mo.
- - - - - *tranflated into German, and increafed Leipzig* 1779, 8vo.

L E I P Z I G.

Briefe eines Sachfen aus der Schweitz an feinen
Freund

Freund. In Leipzig 1785, 1786, 8vo. 3 Th.

BURCKHARDT (JOH. GOTTL.) Bemerkungen auf einer Reise von Leipzig über Frankfurt, Maintz und Oftend bis London. Leipzig, 1783, 8vo,

Reife im Sommer, *vide* BERLIN.

LEYDEN.

ADLER, *vide* AMSTERDAM.

GORIS (GERM) Delices de la campagne a l'entour de la ville de Leyde. A Leyde 1712, 8vo.

LIEGE.

Les delices du païs de Liege. A Liege, 1738, fol. II. tom.

LIPPARI ISLANDS.

DOLOMIEU (DEODAT DE) Voyage aux iſles de Lippari fait en 1781, ou notice fur les iſles Aeoliennes, pour fervir a l' hiſtoire des Volcans fuivi d'un memoire fur une eſpece de Volcan d'air, & un autre fur la temperature du climate de Malthe. A Paris, 1783, 8vo.

The

The same translated into German, by Lichtenberg;
Leipzig, 1783,
HOUEL (JEAN) Voyage pittoresque des isles de Sicile, de Malthe & de Lippari. A Paris 1782, 1783, 1784, fol. XIV. livraisons.

LISBON.

FIELDING'S (HENRY) Journal of a voyage to Lisbon. London, 1755, 8vo.
------ *translated into German, with an account of the life of the author.* Altona, 1764. 8vo.
---------- *Do. into French. A Lausanne* 1783.
KUEHN, *vide* CANARY ISLANDS.

LITHUANIA.

BARDILI, *vide* GERMANY.
GUAGNINO (ALEX.) Sarmatiae Europaeae descriptio, sive Polonia, Lithuania, Russia, Prussia, Pommerania, & Livonia. Cracoviae, 1578, fol.
HERBERSTEIN (SIGISMUND DE) Commentarius de rebus Moscoviticis. Basil. 1556, 1571, fol. Antwerp. 1557, 8vo.
The same translated into German. Basil, 1563, *and Frankf.* 1579, *fol.*
Ditto into Italian. In Venez. 1558, *4to.*

Z   MICHAL-

MICHALONIS, de moribus Tartarorum, Lithuanorum, & Moscorum. Basileae 1615, 4to.

RZACZYNSKY (P. GABR.) Historir naturalis Poloniae, & Magni Ducatus Lithuaniae, &c. Sendomir, 1721, 4to. Cum auctuario Godani, 1736, 4to.

ZEILLER (M.) Beschreibung des Königreichs Pohlen, und des Grosshertzogthums Lithauen. Ulm, 1647, 1652, 8vo.

Ditto, 1657, 8vo.

LITHUANIA (PRUSSIAN).

LEPNER (THEODOR) Preussischer Lithauer, oder Vorstellung der Gebräuche, Sprache, &c. &c. der Lithauer, im Jahr, 1690. Dantzig, 1744, 8vo.

LIVINERTHAL.

SCHINTZ, vide BELLENTZ.

LIVONIA.

BRAND, vide BRANDENBURG.
BOURROUGH's (WILL.) voyage to the Narve in Livonia, in HACKLUYT, vide ANGLESEY.
BURJA, vide COURLAND.
CARLISLE (COMTE DE) vide DENMARK.

De

Defcription de la Livonie, avec le voyage de l'auteur de la Livonie en Hollande, l'an, 1698. A Utrecht, 1705, 8vo.

FISCHER (JAC. BENJ.) Verfuch einer Naturgefchichte von Lifland. Leipz. 1778, gr. 8vo.

FISCHER, *vide* COURLAND.

GUAGNINO, *vide* LITHUANIA.

MAYER, *vide* COURLAND.

OLEARIUS (ADAM) Perfianifche Reyfe door Lyfland, Mofcovien, & Tartaryen. l'Amifterdam, Utrecht, & Groningen, 1651 4to.

STRUYS, *vide* GREECE.

ZEILLER, *vide* FINLAND.

LOMBARDY.

BROWN, *vide* AUSTRIA.

PINI (ERMENEGILDO) dell' elevazione de' principali monti, e di diverfe altre parti della Lombardia Auftriaca. In Milano. 1781, 4to.

LONDON.

BRAZEY, *vide* ENGLAND.

BURCKHARDT, *vide* LEIPZIG.

FABRI, *vide* DALMATIA.

FABRICIUS (JOH. CHR.) Briefe von 1782, aus London. Deffau und Leipzig, 1784. 8vo.   GROSLEY

GROSLEY Londres: Ouvrage d' un François.
A Laufanne, 1768, 1770, 12mo. III tom.
Augmenté de notes d' un Anglois. A.
Neuchatel, 1771, 12mo. III tom.
The fame tranflated from the French, by Nugent,
London, 1772, 8vo. III vol.
PENNANT's (TH.) Journey from Chefter to
London. London, 1782, 4to.
SULIVAN, *vide* EDINBURGH.
VOLTAIRE; Lettres de Londres fur les An-
glois. A Amfterd. 1735. A Oxford,
1771, 8vo.
V. (H. M. D.) memoires, *vide* ENGLAND.

L O R E T T O.

HEIDEGGER, *vide* COMPOSTELLA.

L O R R A I N.

Befchreibung von Lothringen und Savoien,
Nürnberg, 1736, 12mo.
BREVAL, *vide* ALSACE.
DURIVAL (L'AINE) Defcription de la Lor-
raine & du Barrois. A Nancy, 1778,
1779, gr. 4to. III. tom.
KEYSSLER, *vide* BOHEMIA.
LYNAR (GRAF) Reife in Lothringen in BER-
NOULLI'S SAMMLUNG, *vide* AUSTRIA.
R. (COMTE)

R. (COMTE GREGOIRE DE) *vide* CHAMPAIGN.

LUBECK.

AUBERY DE MAURIER, Memoires, *vide* DENMARK.

BREDERODE (REYNH. DE) Jqurnal der legatie naer Mofcovien gedaen 1615 en 1616. Gravenhaag 1619, 4to.

LUCERN (LAKE OF)

CYSATUS (JO. LEOPOLD) Befchreibung des Lucerner Sees. Lucern 1661, 4to.

LUSATIA.

BERNOULLI's Reife in diè Laufnitz im 13ten. & 14 Bändgen feiner Sammlung.
Briefe über Herrnhut, *vide* HERRNHUT.
CAROSI (JOH. PHIL.) Beyträge zur Naturgefchichte der Ober Laufnitz. Leip. 1779.
LESKE (NATH. GOTTFR.) Reife durch Sachfen, Oberlaufnitz in Rückficht der Naturgefchichte und Oeconomie unternommen in 1782. Leipzig, 1785, gr. 4to.
LYNAR (GR. v.) in Bernoulli's Sammlung, *vide* AUSTRIA.

Reife

Reife von Wienn über Prag, *vide* BERLIN.

LUXEMBURGH.

R. (COMTE GREGOIRE DE) *vide* CHAMPAIGN.

LYONNOIS.

DULAC, *vide* BEAUJOLOIS.

MACEDONIA.

BROWN, *vide* AUSTRIA.
LUCAS, *vide* GREECE.

MADEIRA.

ALCAFORADO (FRANC) Relation hiftorique de la decouverte de l'ifle de Madere, traduite du Portugais. A Paris, 1671, 12mo.

The fame translated into *Englifh. London*, 1675, 4to.

Allgemeine Hiftorie der Reifen im 2ten Band, *vide* CANARY ISLANDS.

CONSTANTINI (EMANUEL) infulae Maderae hiftoria. Romae, 1599.

LANDI (GUIL) Defcrizione dell' ifola di Madera, 1574.

MACHAM, voyage to the Ifland of Madeira, in Hackluyt's collection, *vide* ANGLESEY-
OVINGTON'S

OVINGTON's (JOHN) voyage to Surat in the year 1689, &c. with a defcription of the Ifland of Madeira and St. Helena. London, 1698, 8vo.
Tranflated into French. A Paris, 1753, gr. 12mo. II tom.
SLOANE's (SIR HANS) Voyage to the iflands Madeira, &c.

MADRID.

HACKLUYT's 3ter Band, *vide* ANGLESEY.
LOPEZ (THOM) defcription de la provincia de Madrid. Madrid, 1763, 8vo.
Relation de Madrid, ou remarques fur les moeurs de fes habitans. A Cologne, 1665, 12mo.

MAGDEBURGH.

Neue Reifebemerkungen, *vide* BERLIN.

MAJORCA.

CAMPBELL, *vide* FORMENTERA.

MALAGA.

CARTER, *vide* GIBRALTAR.

MALTA.

ABELA (GIOV. FRANC.) Descrizione di Malta, In Malta 1647, fol.

BORCH (COMTE DE) Lettres fur la Sicile & l'isle de Malthe, ecrites en 1777. A Turin, 1782, 8vo. II tom.

The same translated into German. Bern, 1783. 8vo. II Th.

BROWN, *vide* FRANCE.

BRYDONE's (P.) Tour through Sicily and Malta, London, 1773, gr. 8vo. II. vol.

Translated into German. Leipzig. 1777, 8vo. II Th.

Do. into French. A Paris, 1781, 12mo. II vol.

DAPPER, *vide* CANARY ISLANDS.

DOLOMIEU, *vide* LIPPARI ISLANDS.

DRYDEN's (JOHN) voyage to Sicily and Malta, when he accompanied Mr. Cecil in that expedition in 1700—1701. London, 1776, 8vo.

FERDINAND ALBRECHT, *vide* ENGLAND.

HOUEL, *vide* LIPPARI ISLANDS.

M. Letters *vide* ITALY.

MEGISSERI (HIER) propugnaculum Europae. Lips. 1610, 8vo.

MONT (DU) *vide* FRANCE.

NIEDERSTEDT (BURCH) Malta vetus & nova, Helmft, 1666, fo.

PLATIERE, *vide* ITALY.

QUINTINI (Jo.) infulae Melitae defcriptio. Lugd. 1536, 4to.

Reife nach der infel Maltha nebft C. Cordiners Alterthumern, und mahlerifchen Befchreibung von Nord-Schottland. Hamburg, 1783, 8vo.

VERYARD, *vide* FRANCE.

MAN (ISLE OF)

HACKLUYT, *vide* ANGLESEY.

ROLT's hiftory of the ifle of Man from the earlieft account to the prefent time. London, 1773, 8vo.

MANTUA.

VISI (G. B.) notizie ftoriche della cittá e dello ftato di Mantova, 1781, 1784, 4to. II tom.

MARBURG.

Briefe eines Reifenden, *vide* CASSEL.

MARLY.

SAUGRAIN, *vide* St. CLOUD.

MAURA (ST.)

DAPPER, *vide* CEFALONIA.

MECKLENBURG.

Aufzug aus dem Tagebuch eines Ruffen auf feiner Reife von Braunfchweig über Mecklenburg, Pommern, und Preuffen nach Riga, 1783, 8vo.

BERNOULLI's 6ter. Band, *vide* AUSTRIA.
BUCHWALD, *vide* HOLSTEIN.
NUGENT, *vide* GERMANY.

MEDITERRANEAN SEA.

ENS (CASP) Deliciae tranfmarinae, i. e. infignium aliquot maris Mediterranei infularum, portuum, ac maritimorum oppidorum defcriptio. Colon, 1610, 8vo.
MARSIGLI (LUIGI FERD. CONTE) Breve rif-

riftrétto del faggio fifico intorno alla ftoria del mare Mediterraneo, In Venez. 1711, 4to.

SCYLACIS periplus maris Mediterranei, *vide* ASOW.

MENTZ,

BERNOULLI's Sammlung 13ter Band, *vide* AUSTRIA.
BURKHART, *vide* LEIPZIG.
Neue Reifebemerkungen, *vide* BERLIN.

MIDDLESEX.

NORDEN *vide* ENGLAND.

MILAN.

ADLED, *vide* AMSTERDAM.
BOSII (JO. AND.) Hifpaniae, Ducatus Mediolanenfis, & Regni Neapolitani notitia. Helmft. 1702, 4to.
PAVESI (ANGEL) Storia della città e ftato di Milano. In Milano. 1783, 8vo.

MINDEN.

Neue Reifebemerkungen, *vide* BERLIN.

MINORCA.

CLEGHORN's (GEORG) Obfervations on the epidemical difeafes in Minorca, to which is prefixed a fhort account of the climate, productions, inhabitants, and epidemical diftempers of that Ifland. London, 1751, vo.

The fame tranflated into German. Gotha. 1776, 8vo.

Lettres concernantes la defcription d'un voyage fait de Minorque à Rome en l'an 1777 A Frankf. & Leipzig, 1779, 8vo.

LINDEMANN's Befchreibung der Infel Minorca, in FORSTER's und SPRENGEL's Beyträgen zur Völker und Landerkunde. Leipzig, 1786, 8vo. Vter und VIter Theil.

MOLDAVIA.

AVRIL, *vide* EUROPE.
BOSCOWICH, *vide* LEMBERG.

BRONI-

BRONIOVII defcriptio Tartariae. Colon, 1595, fol.

CARRA, hiftoire de la Moldavie & de la Valachie, avec une diſſertation fur l'état actuel de ces provinces. A Paris. 1778, 8vo. I Th.

HACKLUYT's 2d vol. *vide* ANGLESEY.

KANTEMIR (DEMETRIUS) hiftorifche, geographifche, und politifche Befchreibung der Moldau, nebſt dem Leben des Verfaſſers. Frankf. & Leipz. 1778, gr. 8vo.

POSSEVINII (ANT) Mofcovia & alia opera. Colon, 1595. fol.

SULZER (FR. JOS) Gefchicht des Tranfalpinifchen Daciens, d. i. der Wallachey, Moldau, und Beſſarabiens. Wienn 1781, 1782, gr. 8vo.

MONMOUTHSHIRE.

WYNDHAM's tour through Monmouthfhire and Wales. London, 1781, 4to.

MORAVIA.

BERNOULLI, *vide* AUSTRIA.

MOREA

MOREA.

BELLIN, description geographique du Golfe de Venife & de la Morée pour la navigation. A Paris, 1771, 4to. avec XLIX cartes & plans.

Befchreibung des Königreichs Ungarn, und Morea. Frankfurt & Leipzig, 1688, 12mo.

CORONELLI (VINC) Memorie hiftoriografiche dei regni della Morea, Negroponte, e luoghi adjacenti. In Venezia, 1685, 1688, 8vo. II tom.

The fame tranflated into French. A Paris, 1686 8vo. Do. *A Amfterdam*, 1686, 12mo.

Do. into Englifh. London, 1787, 8vo.

DAPPER, vide ARCHIPELAGO.

GROEBEN (OTTO FR. VON DER) Orientalifche Reifebefchreibung, &c. Marienwerder, 1694, 4to.

Neuvermehrte Befchreibung der Halbinfel Morea. Nurnberg, 1637, 8vo. III Th.

PIACENZA, vide ARCHIPELAGO.

P. (D. A P.) Defcrizione, delle provincie, che formano la tanto decantata peninfula della Morea. In Venezia, 1636, 12mo.

The fame translated into German. Nurnberg, 1687, 12mo.

MUNICH.

BIANCONI, *vide* BAVARIA.
BECK's (DOM) Briefe eines Reifenden von Saltzburg durch Munchen und Nurnberg nach Sachfen uber verfchiedene Gegenftände der Naturlehre und Mathematick. Salzburg, 1781, 8vo.

NAPLES:

BARBARO, *vide* ITALY.
BACCO (ENRICO) Regno di Napoli divifo in 12 provincie. In Napoli, 1618, 8vo.
BOSII (Jo. ANT) *vide* MILAN.
BULIFON, *vide* ITALY.
CARACCIOLO (CESARE EUG) Defcrizione del regno di Napoli. In Napoli, 1671, 4to.
FABRICII (GEORG) itinera, Romanum, Neapolitanum, &c. Bafil, 1587, 8vo.
HOUEL, *vide* LIPPARI ISANDS.
MEGISSERI (HIERON) deliciae Neapolitanae. Lips. 1605. 1610, 8vo.
PARRINO (ANT.) Nuovo guida per Napoli. In Napoli, 1725, 12mo.
RIEDESEL (VON) Reife durch Sicilien und Grofs Griechenland. Zurch, 1771, 8vo.
---------- Voyage en Sicile, & dans la Grande Grece, traduit de l' Allemand, accompagné

accompagné de notes du traducteur, Mr. le Comte de Zinzendorf, & du voyage au mont Etna de Monf. de Hamilton. A Laufanne, 1773, 8vo.

--------- travels through Sicily, &c. tranflated by Forſter. London, 1774, 8vo.

SCHOTT: itinerarium *vide* FRANCE.

SHERLOCK, *vide* BERLIN,

SINGLADE, *vide* CORSICA.

SWINBURN's (HENRY) travels into the two Sicilies, 1777, 1780. London, 1783, 4to. vol. I.

TURLERI (HIERONIMI) De peregrinatione, & agro Neapolitano lib. II. Argent, 1574, 12mo. Norimb, 1581, 8vo.

VOLCKARD, *vide* AMSTERDAM.

Voyage pittorefque, ou defcription des Royaumes de Naples & de Sicile. A Paris, 1781, 1783, fol. X chapitres, ou III tom. avec 100 figures.

NASSAU.

FERBER's (JAH. JAC.) Nachrichten von den merkwürdigſten mineraliſchen Gegenden der Hertzoglich Zweybruckiſchen, Churpfalziſchen, Rheingräflichen, und Naſſauiſchen Landen. Mietau, 1776, gr. 8vo,

HABEL's (CHR. FRID) Beyträge zur Naturgefchichte

fchichte, und Oeconomie der Naſſauiſchen Ländern. Deſſau, 1784, 8vo.

NEGROPONT.

CORONELLI, *vide* MOREA.
DAPPER, *vide* ARCHIPELAGO.

NETHERLANDS.

A new traveller's companion through the Netherlands. At the Hague, 1754, 8vo.
A journey through the Auſtrian Netherlands in the year 1724, with an account of all the remarkable battles aud ſieges, &c. London, 1732, 8vo.
BERNOULLI, *vide* AUSTRIA.
BIRKEN, *vide* FRANCE.
BONE (AUG. FRID) Hiſtoriſche, politiſche und geographiſche Beſchreibung der fämtlichen vereinigten Niederlanden. Erf. & Leipz. 1696, 12mo.
BOUSSINGAULT (ADAM) Guide univerſel de tous les Pays Bas. A Paris, 1677, 12mo.
BOXHORNII (ZUERII) epiſtola ad Gabrielem Oxenſtirnium de peregrinatione ejus Batavica. Lugd. 1639, 4to.
Briefe eines reiſenden Franzoſen uber den gegenwärtigen Zuſtand der Oeſterreichiſchen

Niederlanden: Mit einigen Anmerkungen, Verbefferungen, und Zufätzen von Win-kopp. Leipzig, 1785, 8vo. III Th.

BREVAL, *vide* ALSACE.
BROWN, *vide* AUSTRIA.
BURNEY, *vide* BOHEMIA.
BUSCH, *vide* ENGLAND.
CALVETE DE ESTRELLA, *vide* BRABANT.
CELLIUS, *vide* ENGLAND.
CORIAT, curfory remarks, and critical obfervations made upon a journey through part of the Netherlands. London 1766, 12mo. II vol.

CROME (A. F. W.) Statiftifch geographifche Befchreibung der fämtlichen Ofterreichifchen Niederlanden. Deffau und Leipzig, 1785, 8vo.

ELVERI deliciae, *vide* ENGLAND.
ERNDEL, *vide* ENGLAND.
FEBURE, *vide* HOLLAND.

Geographifche und hiftorifche Befchreibung der Niederlanden, aus dem Französifchen von Junckern. Frankfurt 1698, 8vo.

GOELLNIZII Ulyffes Belgico-Gallicus, *vide* FRANCE.

GRAMMAYE (J. B.) peregrinatio Belgica. Coloniae, 1623, 8vo.

HEMPEL, *vide* FRANCE.

HEYSE

HEYSL, *vide* GENOA.

Le voyageur dans les Païs Bas Autrichiens, ou lettres fur l' état actuel de ce päis. A Amfterdam, 1782, 1784, 12mo. VI tom.

Les delices des Païs Bas. A Liege 1689, 8vo. V tom.

M. (C. D. S.) *vide* ALSACE.

MARCELL, *vide* FRANCE.

MARTENE & DURANT, *vide* FRANCE.

MONCONYS, *vide* CONSTANTINOPLE.

NEUMAYR VON RAMSLA, *vide* ENGLAND.[1]

ORTELII itinerarium *vide* FRANCE.

R. (DE LA) *vide* FLANDERS.

RAY, *vide* FRANCE.

Reisbock door de Vereenigte Nederlandfche Provintzen & derfelver aangrenzende Landfchappen & Koningryken. Amfterd. 1700, 8vo.

Remarques hiftoriques, *vide* AUSTRIA.

ROHAN, *vide* ENGLAND.

ROSMITAL, *vide* Do.

SAGITTARII Ulyffes, *vide* Do.

SANDER, *vide* FRANCE.

SCHOCKII (MART) Belgium Foederatum. Amftel. 1652, 12mo.

TEMPLE (WILL) Obfervations on the United Provinces of the Netherlands. London 1673, 8vo.

The fame tranflated into German. Nurnburg, 1676, 12mo.

The

Ditto into French. A. La Haye, 1692, 12mo.

The tour of Holland, *vide* BRABANT.

VBRYARD, *vide* FRANCE.

VOLKMANN's (J. B.) neueste Reisen durch die sieben Vereinigte Provintzen der Niederlanden, vorzuglich in Absicht der Kunst-Sammlungen, Natur Geschichte, Oeconomie, und Manufacturen. Leipzig, 1783, gr. 8vo.

WELSCHEN, *vide* ARCHIPELAGO.

NEUFCHATEL.

BERNOULLI's (JOH) Sammlung kurtzer Reisebeschreibungen 1ter überzähliger Band. Beschreibung des Fürstenthums Welschneuburg und Vallengin. Berlin, 1783, 8vo.

BERNOULLI. *vide* AUSTRIA.

BERTRAND (JEAN ELIE) Description des montagnes & des Vallées, qui font un partie de la principauté de Neufchatel, et Vallengin, 1764, 8vo.

OSTERWALD (FRED) II edition de la description precedente. A Neufchatel, 1766, 8vo.

NICARIA.

GEORGIERENES (JOSEPH) *vide* ATHOS MOUNT.

NORFOLK.

BLOMEFIELD's (FRANC) Essai towards a topographical history of the county of Norfolk. London, 1777, fol. V vol.

NORMANDY.

DUCARE (D.) Anglo Norman antiquities considered in a tour through part of Normandy. London, 1767, 8vo.

SPRENGEL, *vide* ENGLAND.

NORTHERN COUNTRIES.

ADELUNG's (JOH. CHRIST) Geschichte der Schifffahrten und Versuche zur Entdeckung des Nordöstlichen Weges nach Japan und China. Halle 1768, gr. 4to.

Allgemeine Historie der Reisen, *vide* CANARY ISLANDS.

BARRINGTON's Probability of reaching the North Pole, London, 1775, 4to.

BROWN's

BROWN's (ROBERT) ausführliche Beschreibung der See Reise des Ritters Franc. Drake, &c. Leipzig, 1728, 8vo.

BILBERG's voyage of the late King of Sweden, and another of the mathematicians into the Northern parts. London, 1698, 8vo.

CAPEL (RUDOLPH) Norden, oder zu Waſſer und Landezuwege gebrachte Erfahrung und Vorſtellung von Norden. Nebſt Anhang von dem Anfang und Fortgang der Schifffahrt bis auf dieſe Zeit; aus dem Holländiſchen. Hamburg 1678, 4to.

Collection de differens morceaux ſur l'hiſtoire naturelle & civile des pays du Nord, traduite de l'Allemand, du Suedois, & du Latin, avec des notes de Keralio. A Paris, 1763, 12mo.

Eerſte Schipvaert der Hollanders naer Oſtindien door de ſtract van Waigats by Norden, Norwegen, & Moſcovien. Amſterdam, 1648, 4to.

ELLIS (WILL.) authentic narrative of Cook's voyage in the years 1776, 1780. London 1782, 8vo. II vol.

The same translated into German. Frankf. 1783, *gr. 8vo.*

ENGEL (SAM) memoires ſur la navigation dans la mer du Nord depuis le 63 degré de latitude, en allant vers le pole. A Berne 1779, 4to.

HAK-

HAKLUYT, *vide* ANGLESYE.

FORSTER (JOH. REINH.) Gefchichte der Entdeckungen, und Schifffahrt in Norden. Frankf. an der Oder, 1784, 8vo.

HULSII (LEVIN) Sammlung von 26 Schifffahrten der Holländer und Zeelander nach Oft und Weft Indien, wie auch nach Norden. Herausgegeben zu Nurnberg Frankfurt, Oppenheim, und Hanau, 1599, 1650, 4to.

LINSCHOTTEN (JAN HUYGENS VAN) voyagie, of de fhipvaert van Norden omlangs Norwegen, de Noordcap, Lapland, Vinland, Ruffland, de Witte Zee, &c. 1594, 1595. Francker, 1601, fol.

M. (F.) Neuentdecktes Norden, oder Reifebefchreibung in die mitternächtigen und Nordwärts gelegenen Länder. Frankf. und Leipzig 1727, 8vo. Nurnberg, 1728, 8vo.

MAGNI (OLAI) hiftoria de gentibus feptemtrionalibus, earumque diverfis moribus, fuperftitionibus, difciplinis, rebus memorabilibus. Romae 1555. fol. Bafil, 1567, fol. Lugd. Bat. 1645. 12mo. Amfterd. 1669, 12mo.

The fame translated into Italian. In Venezia, 1565, fol.

Do. into German. Bafil, 1567, fol.

MARTINIERE, *vide* GREENLAND.

MEGISSERI (HIERON) Septemtrio novantiquus,

oder

oder die neue Nordwelt. Leipzig 1613, Ditto. 1653, 12mo.

MULLER (JOH. BERNH) Leben und Gewohnheiten der Oftiaken unter dem polo Arctico; nebft einigen Anmerkungen von Königreich Siberien, und dem freto Naffovico. Berlin, 1720, 8vo.

Nouveau recueil des voyages au Nord de l' Europe. A Paris 1785, 8vo. II tom.

OUTHIER vide LAPLAND.

PAGE (DE) voyage du tour du monde, & vers les deux poles, par terre & par mer pendant 1767—1776. A Paris, 1782, 8vo. II tom. A Laufanne & Berne, 1783, 8vo. II vol. A Hambourg 1783, 8vo. II vol.

PALLAS (PETR. SIM) Neue Nordifche Beyträge.

PHIPPS's (CONS. JOHN) Voyage towards the North Pole, in 1773. London, 1774, 4to. *The fame tranflated into German, with additions.* Bern, 1774, 4to.

PICKERSGILL's (RICH) account of voyages for the difcovery of a Northweft paffage. London, 1782, 8vo.

RÖSLIN's (HEINRICH) mitternachtige Schifffahrt von den Herren Staaten in den Niederlanden vergeblich vorgenommen Oppenheim, 1611, 8vo.

SPERLINGII (OTTO) Boreas ejufque laudes. Hafniae, 1696, 8vo.

(V. S. VON)

V. (S. VON) *vide* GREENLAND.
VEER (GERRIT DE) Waeragtige befchryvinge van Will Barents drie feevoyagien &c. — Amfterdam, 1605, 4to.
VOLCKARD, *vide* AMSTERDAM.
WALTHER's (FRID. LUD) neuefte Erdkunde, welche Afien, Africa, Europa, America, die Sud Länder, die Polar Länder, &c. enthält. Nurnberg & Altdorf, 1785, 8vo.
WILLIAM's, *vide* DENMARK.

NORTHAMPTONSHIRE.

MORTON's (THOM) natural hiftory and antiquities of Northamptonfhire. London, 1712, fol,
Sketch of a tour, *vide* BEDFORDSHIRE.

NORTH SEA.

HACKLUYT *vide* ANGLESEY.
KERGUELEN, *vide* FERRO-ISLANDS.
PHIPPS, *vide* NORTHERN COUNTRIES.

NORTHUMBERLAND.

WALLIS, *vide* DURHAM.

NORWAY.

ADAM, vide DENMARK.
BERNHARD, vide Do.
BERNOULLI, vide AUSTRIA.
CAUSSON (PED) Norriges Befcrivelfe. Kiobenh. 1632, 4to.
DASS (PED.) Befcrivelfe over Nordlands Amt, &c. Kiobenh. 1763, 8vo.
ECHOLT (MICH. PETR.) Geologia Norwegiae. Chriftianiae, 1657, 4to.
FABRICIUS (JOH. CHRIST) Reife nach Norwegen mit Bemerkungen aus der Natur-hiftorie und Oeconomie. Hamburg, 1779, 8vo.
GILLEBOEL (RIJERO) naturlig og oeconomifk befkrivelfe over Hölands &c. ftift i Norge. Kiop. 1771, 8vo.
JARS, vide ENGLAND.
JESSEN (ERICH JENS) De Kongerige Norge fremftillet efter dets naturlich og borgerlig tilftand. Kiobenh. 1763, 4to.
JONGE, vide FERRO ISLANDS.
Iftoria naturale vide DENMARK.
KALM, vide ENGLAND.
KERGUELEN, vide FERRO ISLANDS.
MALGO, in HAKLUYT, vide ANGLESEY.
MARTINIERE, vide GREENLAND.
PONTOPPIDAN (ERICH) Förfte forfog paa Norges naturlige hiftorie. Kiobenh. 1752, 4to.

RAMI

RAMI, Norriges befcrivelfe. Kiobenh. 1735, 4to.
RAMUSIO (GIOV. BATT) Raccolte delle navigazioni, &c. In Venezia, 1613, fol. III tom.
Reife vegvifer for Norge. Kiob. 1780. 8vo.
SCHEEL, *vide* DENMARK.
SCHYTTE, *vide* Do.
Tre navigazioni fatte dagli Olandefi e Zelandefi al Settentrione della Norvegia, Mofcovia, e Tartaria. In Venezia, 1599, 4to.
VEER, *vide* NORTHERN COUNTRIES.
WOLF, *vide* GREENLAND.
ZEILLER. *vide* DENMARK.

NOTTINGHAMSHIRE.

Allgemeine hiftorie, *vide* CANARY ISLANDS.
Sketch of a tour, *vide* BEDFORDSHIRE.
THORNTON antiquities of Nottinghamfhire, London, 1677, fol,

NOVA ZEMBLA.

Allgemeine Hiftorie der Reifen, *vide* CANARY ISLANDS.
MARTINIERE, *vide* GREENLAND.
Sammlung mehrerer merkwürdigen Gefchichten zur angenehmen und nützlichen Lecture, Brandenburg, 1783, 8vo.

SCHE-

SCHEMERINGII (DAN) Nova Zembla, five descriptio contracta naviagtionum trium admirandarum a Bélgis per mare Hyperboreum in Chinam & Indiam Orientalem, iter affectantibus, annis supra sesqui mille 94, 95, & 96, irrito conatu tentatarum. Flissingae, 1631, 4to.

ZORGDRAGER, *vide* GREENLAND.

OLAND.

LINNAEUS, *vide* GOTHLAND.

ORENBURG.

RYTSCHKOWA (PET.) topographia Orensburgskaja, &c. St. Petersb. 1762, 8vo. II tom.

The same translated into German. Riga, 1772, 8vo. II Th.

ORKNEY ISLANDS.

JOVII (PAUL) descriptio Brittanniae, Scotiae, Hiberniae, & Orcadum. Basil, 1546.

KERGUELEN, *vide* FERRO ISLANDS.

MALO, in HAKLUYTS, *vide* ANGLESEY.

MARTIN's (M.) description of the western Islands of Scotland, &c. and of Orkney

and

and Shetland. London, 1704, 1716, 8vo.

WALLACE's (JAMES) account of the iflands of Orkney, &c. Edinburgh, 1693, London, 1700.

OXFORDSHIRE.

PLOT's natural hiftory of Oxfordfhire. Oxford, 1677, 1705, fol.

PADUA.

FABRICII itinera, *vide* NAPLES.

PALATINATE.

CASSINI DE THURY, *vide* AUSTRIA.
FERBER, *vide* NASSAU.
Gefammelte Anzeige, *vide* BAVARIA.
Kurtze Vorftellung der Induftrie in den Hauptftädten der Pfalz rückfichtlich auf Manufacturen, Gewerbfchaft und Handlung. Frankenthal, 1775, 8vo.

PARIS.

Almanach du voyageur à Paris & dans les lieux

lieux les plus remarquables du royaume. A Paris, 1780, 12mo.

ANDREWS's (JOHN) Letters to a young Gentleman on his setting out for France, &c, London, 1784, 8vo.

ANTONINI (ABBE) Memorial de Paris, & de fes environs. A Paris, 1742, 12mo.

ARGENVILLE (D) Voyage pittorefque de Paris. A Paris, 1779, 12mo.

BEGUE DE PRELE (ACHILL GUIL) Manuel du naturalifte de Paris, &c. A Paris, 1766 8vo.

Beobachtungen auf einer Reife, *vide* FLANDERS.

BERNOULLI, *vide* AUSTRIA.

DENIS (L.) Itineraire portative. A Paris, 1777, 12mo. III vol.

D. (M.) voyage pittorefque des environs de Paris, ou defcription des maifons Royales, &c. A Paris, 1762, 12mo.

LISTER's (MARTIN) journey to Paris in the year 1698. London, 1699, 8vo.

The fame tranflated into German, with Meintel's remarks. Schwabach, 1753, 8vo.

Luftiges Urtheil über Paris und die Franzofen von einem Sicilianer. Leipzig, 1732, 8vo. Do. 1746, 8vo.

The fame tranflated into Englifh. London, 1749, 8vo.

MERCIER, Tableau de Paris. A Amfterdam, 1783.

1783, 1783, 8vo. VIII tom.
The fame translated into German. Breflau, 1783,
1784, 8vo. IV Bände.
PILATI, vide EUROPE.
SAUGRAIN, vide ST. CLOUD.
SHERLOCK, vide BERLIN.
The tour of Holland, vide BRABANT.

P A S S A U.

SCHRANK, vide AUSTRIA.
Tagebuch eines Hofmeisters, vide BAVARIA.

P A T M O S.

DAPPER, vide ARCHIPELAGO.
GEORGIERENES, vide ATHOS MOUNT.

PELOPONESUS.

PIACENZA, vide ARCHIPELAGO.

PETERSBURG.

BELL'S (DR. JOHN) Reisen von Petersburg in verschiedene Gegenden Asiens, &c.
— — — — Travels into Russia, II vol. 8vo. and II vol. 4to.

DE-

DESCHISAUX (PIERRE) Defcription d'un voyage fait à St. Peterfburg, en 1727. A Paris, 1728, 8vo.

Kleine Reifen, *vide* COLOGNE.

WRAXALL, *vide* COPENHAGEN.

PIEDMONT.

A brief account of the Vaudois, His Sardinian Majefty's proteftant fubjects in the vallies of Piedmont. London, 1753, 8vo.

Viaggio d' un uomo qualificato, *vide* ENGLAND.

PILATE (MOUNT OF)

TOURETTE (DE LA) Voyage au mont Pilate dans la province du Lyonnois, contenant des obfervations fur l' hiftoire naturelle de cette montagne. A Avignon, 1770, 8vo.

PISTOJA.

MATANI (ANT.) relazione iftorica e filofofica delle produzioni naturali del territorio Piftojefe. In Piftoja, 1762, 4to. In Venezia, 1779, 4to.

PO-

POLAND.

AUBERY, *vide* DENMARK.
AUSTEL, IN HAKLUYT, *vide* ANGLESEY.
BARDILI, *vide* GERMANY.
BEAUJEU, *vide* Do.
BERNOULLI, *vide* AUSTRIA.
BERNOULLI, *vide* BELLUNO.
BEYRLIN, *vide* GERMANY.
BOSCOWICH, *vide* BULGARIA.
CAROSI (JOH. PHIL. VON) Reife durch verfchiedene Polnifche Provintzen; mineralogifchen und andern Inhalts. Leipz. 1781, 1784. II Th. 8vo.
CHROMER, *vide* HUNGARY.
COXE, *vide* DENMARK.
ELVERI (HIERON) *vide* ENGLAND:
GUAGNINO, *vide* LITHUANIA.
HAKLUYT, *vide* ANGLESEY.
HAUTEVILLE; Relation hiftorique de la Pologne. A Paris, 1687, 12mo.
HEBERER VON BRETTEN, *vide* DENMARK.
HERBERSTEIN. *vide* LITHUANIA.
JÖSTEN, *vide* AUSTRIA.
Journal van het gefandfchap op den vredehandel tufchen Pohlen & Sweden, 1627, 1632.
L. (DE) *vide* GERMANY.

LOMENII Itinerarium, *vide* AUSTRIA.
MARSHALL, *vide* DENMARK.
MOTRAYE (A. DE LA) Travels in several countries of Pruffia, Ruffia, and Poland. London & Dublin, 1732, fol.
OGERI ephemerides, *vide* DENMARK.
PAYEN, *vide* BRABANT.
REGNARD, *vide* DENMARK.
RZACZYNSKY, *vide* LITHUANIA.
VIAGGII d' un uomo qualificato, *vide* ENGLAND.
VIGENERE (BLAISE DE) Defcription du royaume de Pologne. A Paris, 1573, 4to.
WILLIAMS, *vide* DENMARK.
ZEILLERS, *vide* LITHUANIA.

POMERANIA.

APELBLAD, *vide* BRANDENBURGH.
AUSZUG aus dem Tagebuch, *vide* MECKLENBURGH.
BERNOULLI, *vide* COURLAND.
BRUIGGEMAN's (L. W.) ausführliche Befchreibung, und gegenwärtiger Zuftand von Vor und Hinter Pommern. Stettin, 1779, 1784, gr. 4to. II Th.
BUCHWALD, *vide* HOLSTEIN.
GUAGNINO, *vide* LITHUANIA.
ZEILLER, *vide* GERMANY.

POPE'S DOMINIONS.

MAIRE & BOSCOWICH, Voyage aftrono-
mique & geographique dans l'etat de l'
Eglife, pour mefurer deux degrés du me-
ridien, & corriger la carte de l' Etat Ecclefiaftique. A Paris, 1770, 4to.
The fame in Bernoulli's archiv, vide BEL-
LUNO.

PORTUGAL.

BARETTI, *vide* ENGLAND.
BROCKWELL (C.) natural and political hiftory
of Portugal. London, 1726, 8vo.
BROME, *vide* ITALY.
BURGE (WILL VAN DER) nieuwe hiftorifche
geographifche, reifbefchryving van Spanien, en Portugal. Gravenhaag, 1705,
4to. II deele.
COLMENAR (JUAN ALVAREZ DE) Delices d'
Efpagne & de Portugal. A Leide, 1707,
1715, 12mo. VI tom.

Sous,

-------- Sous le titre: Annales d'Espagne, &c. Amsterdam, 1741, 4to. IV tom. Do. 8vo. VIII tom.

CRONE, vide EUROPE.

DALRYMPLE's (WILL) Travels through Spain and Portugal, in 1774. London, 1777, 4to.

The same translated into German, with remarks. Leipz. 1778, 8vo.

Der Schauplatz von Spanien und Portugal. Amsterd. 1704, 12mo.

DRAKE IN HACKLUYT, vide ANGLESEY.

Etat present du royaume de Portugal en 1766. A Lausanne, 1775, 12mo.

FARIA (SEVERIN) Noticias de Portugal. Lisboa, 1740, fol.

FIELDING, vide LISBON.

GOES (DAMIANI DE) Legatio Magni Indorum Imperatoris, Presbyteri Ioannis ad Emannuelem, Lusitaniae Regem, 1513. Dordraci, 1618, 12mo.

HERVEY, vide GERMANY.

HONTAN, vide DENMARK.

LAET (Jo.) Hispania, &c. Lugd. Bat. 1629, 16mo.

Letters on Portugal, on the present and former state of that Kingdom. London, 1777, 8vo.

The same translated into French. A Paris, 1780.

Do.

Do. into German, with remarks, by Sprengel,
Leipz. 1782, 8vo.

M. voyage, *vide* FRANCE.

MONCONYS, *vide* CONSTANTINOPLE.

Merckwürdigkeiten von Portugal. Frankf. und Leipz. 1777, IV Stuck.

NUNEZ (EDWARDO) Defcripçao do Reyno de Portugal. Lifboa, 1610, 4to.

Remarques d' un voyageur, *vide* GERMANY.

RESENDII (AND) deliciae Lufitanico-Hifpanicae. Colon. Agripp. 1613, 8vo.

RODEN VEL LIMBERG, *vide* ENGLAND.

S. (   ) voyage, *vide* FRANCE.

SINCERI (EMAN.) Befchreibung von Spanien und Portugal. Naumb. 1700, 12mo.

SPRENGEL, *vide* ENGLAND.

TWISS (RICH.) travels through Portugal and Spain. London, 1775, 4to.

The fame tranflated into German, with remarks, by Ebeling. Leipzig, 1776, 8vo.

Do. into French. A Berne, 1776, 8vo.

UDAL AP RHYS's (   ) account of the moft remarkable places and curiofities in Spain and Portugal. London, 1740, 1760, 8vo.

VAL (PIERRE DU) Defcription & l' alphabet d' Efpagne, & de Portugal, &c. 1666, 12mo.

Voyages faits, *vide* GERMANY:

WIN-

WINGFIELD IN HAKLUYT, *vide* ANGLESEY.
ZEILLERI (MART.) itinerarium Hispaniae & Lusitaniae. Amsterd. 1656, 12mo.
The same translated into German. Amsterd. 1650, 12mo.

POTSDAM.

Neue Reisebemerkungen, *vide* BERLIN.
Reise im Sommer, *vide* Do.
Reise von Wienn, *vide* Do.

PRAGUE.

Reise von Wienn, *vide* BERLIN.

PRESBURG.

FRIEDEL's (JOH) Briefe aus Wienn. Leipzig, 1783, 8vo.
LAHMAN *vide* HERMANSTADT.

PROVENCE.

BERENGER voyage en Provence. A Marseille & Orleans, 1783, 12mo.
—————Soirées provençales. A Paris, 1786, 12mo. III tom.
DURLAC (   ) Histoire naturelle de la Provence

vence. A Avignon & Marseille, 1783,
8vo. II tom.

GIRAUD SOULAVIE, vide AUVERGNE.

GRASSERI itinerarium, vide ITALY.

Kleine Reisen, vide ERMENONVILLE.

MONCONYS vide CONSTANTINOPLE.

PAPON (JEAN PIERRE) Voyage litteraire de la Provence. A Paris, 1780, gr. 12mo.

The same translated into German, with remarks. Leipzig, 1783, 8vo.

Relation d'un voyage fait en Provence. A Paris, 1683, 12mo.

P R U S S I A.

Aufzug aus dem Tagebuch eines Russen, vide MECKLENBUBGH.

Bemerkungen auf einer Reise von Berlin nach Bromberg in West Preussen. Berlin und Leipzig, 1784, 8vo.

BENJAMINIS NAVARRENI itinerarium, vide EUROPE.

BERNOULLI, vide COURLAND.

BERNOULLI's Archiv, vide BELLUNO.

BOCK's (FRID. SAM) Versuch einer wirthschaftlichen Naturgeschichte von dem Königreich Ost und West Preussen. Dessau, 1782. 1784, 8vo. IV Th.

BRAND, vide BRANDENBURG.

BURJA

BORJA, *vide* COURLAND.
GUAGNINO, *vide* LITHUANIA.
HACKLUYT, *vide* ANGLESEY.
KUESTER (CARL DAN) Kleine Preufifche Länder Kentnüfs. Magdeburg und Deffau, 1782, 8vo. II Th.
LEPNER, *vide* PRUSSIAN LITHUANIA.
MARSHALL *vide* DENMARK.
MANGELSDORF (K. E.) Preuffiche national Blätter. Hall, 1787, 8vo.
MOTRAYE, *vide* POLAND.
STELLA (ERASMUS) De Boruffiae antiquitatibus

PYRENEAN MOUNTAINS.

ARCET (D.) Difcours fur l'état naturel des montagnes des Pyrenées, & fur les caufes de leur degradation. A Paris, 1776, 8vo.
The fame tranflated into German. Berlin, 1779, 8vo.
ROI (LE) Memoires fur les travaux, qui ont rapport a l'exploitation de la nature dans les Pyrenées. Londres & Paris, 1776, 4to.

RAGUSA.

AUSTEL in Hackluyt, *vide* ANGLESEY.

RHINE

RHINE COUNTRIES.

COLLINI (COSME) Journal d' un voyage dans le cercle du Rhin, qui contient differentes obfervations mineralogiques, particuliere- ment fur les agates & les bafaltes ; avec un detail fur la maniere de travailler les agates. A Manheim 1776, 8vo. A Paris 1777, 8vo.

The fame translated into German. Manheim, 1777, 8vo.

GERKEN, *vide* BAVARIA.

HAMILTON's neuere Beobachtungen über die Volcanen, *vide* ITALY.

HUPSCH (J. W. K. A.) FREYHERR VON) mah- lerifche Reife am Nieder Rhein. Cölln, 1784, 1785, gr. 4to. II Hefte.

Remarques hiftoriques, *vide* BOHEMIA.

RHODUS.

BRUYN, *vide* CYPRUS.

CORONELLI (VINC) Ifola di Rodi geografica, ftorica, antica, e moderna, &c. In Venezia, 1688, 8vo.

DAPPER, *vide* ARCHIPELAGO,

SOMMER, *vide* Do.

RIESENGEBURG.

Die wunderbahre Schneekoppe, oder Befchreibung des Riefengebürges. Leipzig, 1746, 8vo.

Reifen auf das Schlefifche Riefengebürg von 1696. bis 1737. Hirfchberg, 1737, 4to.

VOLKMAR (JOH. JAC) Reifen nach dem Riefengeburg. Bunzlau, 1777, 8vo.

RIGA.

Aufzug aus dem Tagebuch, *vide* MECKLENBURG.

ROME.

ADLER, *vide* AMSTERDAM.

ADLER (JNC) Reifebemerkungen auf einer Reife nach Rom. Altona, 1784, 8vo.

BASSANI (ANT.) Viaggio a Roma della Sacra Real Maefta di Maria Cafimira, Regina di Polonia, per il voto di vifitare i luoghi fanti, ed il fupremo paftore della Chiefa, Innocenzo XII. In Roma, 1700, 4to.

BAUR's

BAUER's (A. F.) Ausführliche Geschichte der Reise des Pabst Pius VI. von Rom nach Wienn, &c. Wienn, 1782, 1783, 8vo. III Th.

BERNOULLI, vide AUSTRIA.

Briefe auf einer Reise nach Rom, &c. 1773, 1774, aus dem Französischen. Riga, 1784, 8vo. II Th.

De trium Regum Japonicorum legatis, qui Roman profecti, Gregorio XIII obedientiam publice praestiterunt. Antw. 1593, 8vo.

FABRICII itinera, vide NAPLES.

FICORONI (FRANC. DE) Offervazioni sopra l'antichitá di Roma. In Roma, 1709, 4to.

FONTANA (BARTH.) Viaggio da Venezia a Roma. In Venezia 1550, 8vo.

GUALTIERI (GUIDO) Relazione della venuta degli Ambasciatori Giaponesi a Roma, &c. In Venezia, 1586, 8vo.

The same translated into German. Dillingen, 1587, 8vo.

Kleine Reisen, vide ERMENONVILLE.

LETI (GREG) itinerario della Corte di Roma &c. In Valenza, 1675, 12mo. III vol.

NODOT, vide ITALY.

Relazione della solenne entrata fatta in Roma da (Fil. Franc) Faxicura, Ambasciatore del Idate Masamune, Ré di Voxu nel Giapone

pone alla Santitia di N. S. Papa Paolo V. In Roma, 1615, 4to.

The fame tranflated into Spanifh. En Mexico, 1626, 8vo.

Do. from the Japanefe language into Latin, by Edward de Sandé. At Macao, 1690, 4to.

SEBASTIANI (DE) Viaggio curiofo di Roma facra e piofana. In Roma, 1683, 12mo.

SHERLOCK, vide BERLIN.

SINGLADE, vide CORSICA.

SPRENGEL, vide ENGLAND.

STUNICAE (LAPIDIS) Itinerarium ab Hifpania ufque ad Romam. Romae, 1521, 4to.

SULIVAN, vide EUROPE.

ROMANIA.

BOSCOWICH, vide BULGARIA.

RONCA.

FORTIS (ALB) Della valle Vulcanico—marina nel territorio Veronefe memoria orytogra, fica. In Venezia, 1778, 4to.

The fame translated into German. Heidelberg, 1779, 8vo.

RUSSIA.

A Journey through Ruffia into Perfia, by two Englifh Gentlemen. London, 1742, 8vo.

ALGAROTTI (CONTE D') Saggio di lettere fopra la Ruffia. In Parigi, 1760, 8vo.

The fame tranflated into French. A Londres, & Paris, 1769, 12mo. *Neufchatel,* 1770, 8vo.

Do. into Englifh. London, 1769, 8vo II vol.

Allgemeine Gefchiche der neueften Entdeckungen, welche von verfchiedenen gelehrten Reifenden in vielen Gegenden des Ruffifchen Reichs, &c. in der Hiftorie, Landwirthfchaft, und Naturgefchichte find gemacht worden. Bern, 1777, 1782, 8vo. V Th.

The fame tranflated into French. A Bern, 1779.

AVRIL, *vide* EUROPE.
BARDILS, *vide* GERMANY.
BELL, *vide* PETERSBURGH.
BERNOUILLI, *vide* COURLAND.
- - - - - - *vide* AUSTRIA.
BRAND (ADAM) Befchreibung feiner groffen Chinefifchen Reifen, &c. Frankfurt, 1697, 8vo. Lubeck, 1734, 8vo.

The same translated into French. Amsterdam, 1699, 12mo.

Do. into Dutch. Tyel, 1699, 8vo.

BRAND, *vide* BRANDENBURG.

BRUCE, *vide* GERMANY.

BRUYN (CORN. VAN) Reisen pver Moscovien Delft, 1714, fol.

The same translated into French. A la Haye, 1732, 4to. *V tom.*

Do. into English. 1737, *fol. II vol.*

BURJA, *vide* COURLAND.

CARLISLE, *vide* DENMARK.

Cook's voyage and travels through the Russian Empire, in 1739, 1750. Edinburgh, 1770, 8vo.

COXE, *vide* DENMARK.

DOES, *vide* CONSTANTINOPLE.

GEISLER, *vide* FRANCE.

GEORGI's (JOH. GOTTL) Bemerkungen auf einer Reise im Russischen Reiche von 1772, 1774.

— — — — — Beschreibung aller Nationen des Russischen Reichs; in 4 Aufgaben. St. Petersburg, 1760. 1780, gr. 4to.

The same translated into Russian. St. Petersburgh, 1776, 1780, 4to. *IV tom.*

Do. into French. St. Petersbourg, 1776, 4to. *IV collections.*

GMELIN's (SAM. GOTTL) Reisen durch Russland zu Untersuchung der 3 Naturreiche St. Pe-

St. Peterſburg, 1770, 1774, 1784, gr. 8vo,
IV Th.
Tranſlated into Ruſſian. St. Peterſburg, 1771,
1774, 4to. *III tom.*
GOETCERI'S JOURNAL, *vide* DENMARK.
HACKLUYT, *vide* ANGLESEY.
HANWEY, *vide* GERMANY.
HERBERSTEIN, *vide* LITHUANIA.
HERFER's (D. A.) Schiffreiſe nach Rufsland,
1677. Nurnberg, 1678, 4to.
HERMAN, *vide* FINLAND.
Hiſtoriſch verhael, of beſchryving van de
voyage gedaen onder de ſuite van den
Heer Coenrad van Klenk extraordinari
Ambaſſadeur van H.H.M. de Heeren Staaten General aan Syn Zaarſche Majeſteyt,
t' Amſterdam, 1677, 4to.

JACOBI, hodoeporicon Ruthenicum, in quo de
Moſcovitarum regione, moribus, religione,
gubernatione, & aula, &c. Francof. 1608, 4to.
JOSTEN, *vide* AUSTRIA.
JOVIUS (PAUL) Beſchreibung der Geſandſchaft
des Ruſſiſchen Fürſten Baſilii M. an den
Pabſt Clemens VII. Baſel, 1537, fol.
The ſame tranſlated into Latin. Baſil. 1551, fo.
Iſtoria naturale, *vide* DENMARK.
JUSTICE's voyage to Ruſſia. York, 1739,
8vo.

RORSII

Korbii (Joh. Georg.) Diarium itineris in Moscoviam Ignatii Christophori de Guarient & Rall a Leopoldo ad Czarum Moscoviae Petrum Alexiovicium, 1698, ablegati extraordinarii. Accessit-reditus Czareae Majestatis, rebellionis Streliziorum, & praecipuarum Moscoviae rerum descriptio. Viennae, 1760, fol.

Lesechina (Iwana) dnewnija sapiski putcá scheftwija po rasn 6m provintzijam Rossijskagho Ghosudarstwa, 1768, i 1769, ghodu. W. Sanckt-Petersburghje, 1771, 4to. 1781, 4to.

The same translated into German. Altenburg, 1774, 1776, 1782, gr. 4to. III Th.

Letters from a Lady who resided some years in Russia. London, 1775, 8vo.

The same translated into German. Leipzig, 1775, 8vo.

Do. into French. A Rotterdam, 1776, 8vo.

Levesque ( ) Histoire de differens peuples soumis à la domination des Russes, A Paris, 1783, II tom.

Lyseck (Adolph) Relatio eorum, quae circa Sacrae Caes. Majest. ad Magnum Moscorum Tzarum legatos Annib. Franc. de Bottoni, & Johannem Carolum Terlingerum anno 1675 gesta sunt. Salisb. 1676, 8vo. Mogunt. 1679, 1689, 8vo.

Mal-

MALHAUT, Essai sur le commmerce de Russie, avec l' histoire de ses decouvertes. A Amsterdam, 1777, 8vo.

MARCY(ABBE)Histoire moderne des Chinois &c. A Paris, 1765, 1778, XXX vol. gr. 12mo.

MARSHALL, *vide* DENMARK.

MARTINIERE, *vide* GREENLAND.

MAYERBERG (AUG. DE) Descriptio itineris, sui, & Horat Guil. Calvuccii ab Imperatore Leopoldo ad Czarum Alexium Michaelowitz ablegatorum in Moscoviam; cum statutis Moscoviticis, ex Russo in Latinum idioma ab ipso translatis. Colon. 1663 fol.

The same translated into French. A *Leide*, 1638, *gr.* 12*mo.*

MEYER'S (J. H. C.) Briefe über Rufsland. Göttingen, 1778, 1779, 8vo. II Th.

MICHALONIS fragmenta de moribus Tartarorum, *vide* LITHUANIA

Moscovitische Land--Zeit—Staats und Kirchenbeschreibung. Nurnberg, 1687.

MOTRAYE, *vide* POLAND.

NEUVILLE en Hez, *vide* CRIM.

NEUGEBAUERI (SALOM) Moscovia, h. e. de origine, situ, regionibus, religione, ac republica Moscoviae. Gedani, 1612, 1613, 4to.

NIEUSTAD (N) Reisebeschryving van Pohlen na Moscovien, 1689. Tyel, 1699, 8vo.

OLEARIUS (ADAM)Moscovitische Beschreibung

F f   der

der Reife nach Mofcow, &c. Schlefwig, 1647, fol.

The fame tranflated into French. A Paris, 1659, 4to.
Do. into Englifh. London, 1662, fol

PALLAS (P. S.) Reifen durch verfchiedene Provintzen des Ruffifchen Reichs in 1768, 1773. Peterfburg 1771, 1773, 1776, gr. 4to. III Theil.

PERRY's (CHARLES) Prefent ftate of Ruffia. London, 1716, 8vo.
Tranflated into German. Leipzig, 1717, 8vo.

PETREJUS (PEHR) Regni Mofcovitici defcriptio. Stockholm, 1615, 4to.

POSSEVINII (ANT.) Mofcovia, five narratio de moribus magnae Ruflorum monarchiae, &c. Dantifci, 1670, 4to.

POTOKI (PAUL) Mofcovia, five narratio de moribus magnae Ruflorum monarchiae &c. Dantifci, 1670, 4to.

PRINZ BARO A BUCHAU (DANIEL) Bis legati Maximiliani IIdi & Rudolphi II ad Johannem Bafilidem Mofcoviae ortus & progreffus. Gubenae, 1679, 4to. Do. 1681, 12mo.

PURCHAS (SAM.) pilgrims. London, 1626, fol. IV vol.

PURGOLD (JOH) De diverfis imperii Ruffici ordinibus eorumque juribus & divinationibus necnon de diverfis foris competentibus. Hallae, 1785, 8vo.

RANDOLPH, *vide* DENMARK.

RAMUSIO

RAMUSIO, Raccolte delle navigazioni e viaggi, &c. In Venezia, 1613, fol. III tom.

Reifebefchryvinge door Vrankryk, *vide* ENGLAND.

Rerum Mofcoviticarum auctores varii ex collectione Freheri. Francof, 1600, fol.

Ruffia, feu Mofcovia, itemque Tartaria commentario topographico atque politico illuftrata. Lugd. Bat. 1630, 16mo.

RYTSCHKOWA (NICOLAJA) Zehurnal ili dnewn üja zapifki putefcheftwija porazn üm provintzijam Roffijfkagho Ghofudarftwa, 1769, 1770, ghoda. Sanct. Peterfburghje, 1770, 4to.

‐ ‐ ‐ ‐ ‐ ‐ Predolzchenic zfckurnala ili dnewn uch zapifk' putefcheftwija po rafn üm provintziam Rofsyfkagho Ghofudarftwa 1770, ghodw. Sanct. Peterfburghje, 1722, 4to.

‐ ‐ ‐ ‐ ‐ ‐ ‐ dewn üja zapifki putefchewija w kirgis Kaifazkoi ftepje 1771, ghodu, Sanct. Peterfburghje, 1772, 4to.

‐ ‐ ‐ ‐ ‐ ‐ ‐ *tranflated into German*. Riga, 1774, 8vo.

SPRENGEL, *vide* ENGLAND.
STRAHLENBERG, *vide* EUROPE.
STRUYS, *vide* GREECE.
TANNERI (BERN. LEOP. FRANC) Legatio Polonico—Lithuanica in Mofcoviam, 1678 fufcepta. Norib. 1689, 4to.

Topografitfchefkija primijitfchanü na znantniefchija mjefta putefcheftwija Eja Imperatorfkagho welitfcheftwa W. Bjelorufkija Namjeftwitfchefwa w Sanct Peterfburghje, 1780, 12mo.

Tre navigazioni fatte da' Olandefi, *vide* NORWAY.

Uber Rufsland. Breflau, 1781, 8vo.

ULFELDI (JACOB) Legatio Mofcovitica. Francof. 1622, 4to.

VEER, *vide* NORTHERN COUNTRIES.

Viaggi di Mofcovia delli anni 1633, 1635. In Viterbo, 1658, 4to.

WARTIS (GIOU.) Relazione geografica ftorico-politica dell imperio di Mofcovia. In Milano, 1713, 12mo.

WICKHART'S (CARL VALENT) Mofcovitifche Reifebefchreibung, und Gefandfchaft nach Mofcau. Wien, 1675, 12mo.

WILLIAMS *vide* DENMARK.

WENZEL'S (D. VON) gegenwärtiger ftaat von Rufsland. Peterfburg und Leipzig, 1783.

The fame translated into French. A Peterfburg & Leipzig, 1783, 8vo.

WREECH (CURT. FRID. VON) Umftändliche Hiftorie von den Schwedifchen Gefangenen in Rufsland, und Siberien. Sorau, 1728, 8vo.

SALTZ.

SALTZBURG.

BERNOULLI, *vide* AUSTRIA.
GERKEN, *vide* BAVARIA.
HERMANN, *vide* AUSTRIA.
SCHRANK, *vide* Do.

SAMOS.

DAPPER, *vide* ARCHIPELAGO.
GEORGIERENES, *vide* ATHOS MOUNT.

SARDINIA

CETTI (FRANC) Storia naturale di Sardegna. In Saſſari 1774—1777—1784, 8vo. III tom.
The same tranſlated into German, and increaſed by Pietſch. Leipz. 1783, 8vo.
Deſcription géographique, hiſtorique, & politique du royaume de Sardaigne. A Cologne, 1718, 8vo. A la Haye, 1725, 12mo.
FUES's Nachrichten aus Sardinien von der gegenwärtigen Verfaſſung dieſer Inſel. Leipzig, 1780, 8vo.
GEMELLI (FRANC) Rifiorimento della Sardegna:

degna. In Saffari, 4to. II tom.
VICO (FRANC. DE) Hiftoria general de la ifla y reyno de Cerdêna. En Barcelona, 1639, fo. II vol.
WELSCHEN, vide ARCHIPELAGO.

S A V O Y.

BREVAL, vide ALSACE.
COULON, vide FLANDERS.
GOELNIZII Ulyffes, vide FRANCE.
LUC, vide ALPS.
POCOCKE, vide ARCHIPELAGO.
R. (DE LA) vide FLANDERS.

S A X O N Y.

ANDROPHILI, vide FRANCONIA.
APELBLAD (JONAS) vide HESSE.
BARTII (MICH.) Hodoeporicon, feu iter Saxonicum. Leipf. 1563, 12mo.
BERNOULLI, vide AUSTRIA.
BECK, vide MUNICH.
Briefe über Sachfen von einem Reifenden. Berlin, 1768, 8vo.
BUCHER, vide DRESDEN.
BURNEY, vide BOHEMIA.
FALCKERT's (ABR. GOTTL) Reifen aus Sachfen bis in Weft-Indien. Budiffin, 1735, 8vo.

LEH-

LEHMANN's (CHRIST.): Hiftorifcher Schau-
platz der natürlichen Merkwürdigkeiten
in dem Meifsnifchen Ober Ertzgebürge.
Leipzig, 1699, 4to. 1747.
LESKE's (NATH. GOTTF.) *vide* LUSATIA.
Mahlerifche Reife' durch Sachfen. Leipzig,
1786, fol. mit XI Kupffern.
Neue Reifebefchreibungen, *vide* BERLIN.
Remarques hiftoriques, *vide* AUSTRIA.
UFFENBACH, *vide* ENGLAND.
VOLCKARD, *vide* AMSTERDAM.
WILL, *vide* ALTDORFF.

SCHAFHAUSEN.

BERNOULLI, *vide* AUSTRIA.

THE SCHWARTZWALD,
or, BLACK FOREST.

BERNOULLI, *vide* AUSTRIA.
Befchreibung einer Reife durch einen kleinen
Theil des Schwartzwaldes, in 6 Briefen
an einen Freund. Franf. 1781, gr. 8vo.

SCILLY ISLANDS.

BORLASE's (WILL.) State of the iflands of
Scilly, 1756, 4to.

SCIO

SCIO.

BRUYN, *vide* CYPRUS.
HACKLUYT, *vide* ANGLESEY.

SCLAVONIA.

BLOUNT, *vide* DALMATIA.
CHROMER'S, *vide* HUNGARY.
PILLER & MITTERBACHER, iter per Pofeganam, Sclavoniae provinciam fufceptum. Budae, 1783, 4to. cum XVI fig.
TAUBE (FRID. WILH. JOH.) Befchreibung des Königreichs Sclavonien und Hertzogthums Syrmien. Leipzig & Wienn, 1777, 1778, 8vo. III Th.

SCOTLAND.

A tour through the whole ifland of Great-Britain, *vide* ENGLAND.
A journey through Scotland. London 1723, 8vo. III vol.
A journey through England, &c. *vide* ENGLAND.
A journey through part of England, *vide* ENGLAND.

B. (R.) *vide* ENGLAND.
ANDERSON, *vide* HEBRIDES.
BEVERELL, *vide* ENGLAND.
BERKENHOUT, *vide* Do.
BROME, *vide* Do.
CAMPBELL, *vide* Do.
CHILDRY, *vide* Do.
CORDINER (CHARLES) Antiquities and fceneries of the North of Scotland. London, 1780. 4to.
DOUGLAS (FRANC.) general defcription of the Eaft coaft of Scotland from Edinburgh to Cullen. London, 1782, 12mo.
DRAYTON. *vide* ENGLAND.
ENS, *vide* Do.
GORDON, *vide* Do.
HERMANNIDAE Brittannia, *vide* Do.
JARS, *vide* Do.
JOVII defcriptio, *vide* Do.
JOHNSON, *vide* HEBRIDES.
Journey to the Highlands of Scotland, with occafional remarks on Dr. Johnfon's tour, by a lady. London, 1779, 8vo.
Journey through England. &c. *vide* ENGLAND.
LELAND, *vide* ENGLAND.
Letters from a gentleman in the North of Scotland to his friend in London. London, 1756, 8vo. II vol.

The same translated into German. Hanover, 1760. 1776, gr. 8vo. II Th.

LITHGOW, *vide* EUROPE.

MARTIN, *vide* ORKNEY ISLANDS.

MISSON, *vide* ENGLAND.

Observations made, *vide* ENGLAND.

PENNANT (THOM.) Tour in Scotland, 1769. London 1774, 4to.

Additions on the quarto edition. London, 1774, 4to.

RAY's (JOHN) Select remains. London, 1760, 8vo.

ROHAN, *vide* ENGLAND.

Sammlung der besten und neuesten Reisebeschreibungen, *vide* CYPRUS.

SIBBALDI (ROBERTI) Scotia illustrata, seu prodromus historiae naturalis Scotiae. Edinburgh, 1684, fol.

‑ ‑ ‑ ‑ ‑ ‑ ‑ ‑ ‑ Nuntius de Atlante Scotico, seu descriptio Scotiae antiquae & modernae. Edenb. 1683.

‑ ‑ ‑ ‑ ‑ ‑ ‑ ‑ History ancient and modern of the Sheriffdom of Fife. &c. Edinb. 1710.

STUKELEY, *vide* ENGLAND.

SULIVAN, *vide* EDINBURGH.

The modern universal British traveller, *vide* ENGLAND.

Tour through Great-Britain, *vide* ENGLAND.

VOLKMANN's neueste Reisen durch Schottland, *vide* IRELAND.

YOUNG

YOUNG, *vide* ENGLAND.
ZEILLER, *vide* Do.

S E R V I A.

BROWN, *vide* AUSTRIA.

SHETLAND ISLANDS.

Journey to the Highlands, *vide* SCOTLAND.
KERGUELEN, *vide* FERRO ISLANDS.
MARTIN, *vide* ORKNEY ISLANDS.

S I C I L Y.

BENJAMINIS NAVARRENI ITINERARIUM, *vide* EUROPE.
BERNOULLI's Archiv, *vide* BELLUNO.
BISCARI (IGNAZIO PATERNO PRENCIPE DI) viaggio per tutta l' antichitá della Sicilia. In Napoli, 1781, 4to.
BORCH, *vide* MALTA.
BRYDONE, *vide* Do.
CARTANI, Reife in Sicilien in Bernoulli's Sammlung, *vide* AUSTRIA.
DRYDEN, *vide* MALTA.
FACELLI (THOM.) De rebus Siculis decades II. Pan-

II. Panormi, 1558, fol. Francof. 1579, fol.

HOUEL, *vide* LIPPARI ISLANDS.

KUSELII itinerarium, *vide* GERMANY.

Lettres fur la Sicile par un voyageur Italien, en 1776—1777. A Amſterdam & Paris, 1778, 12mo.

M. Lettres, *vide* ITALY.

MONGITORE (ANT.) La Sicilia ricercata nelle cofe le piu memorabili. In Palermo, 1742, II tom.

PILATI, *vide* EUROPE.

PLATIERE, *vide* ITALY.

RIEDESEL. *vide* NAPLES.

SESTINI (DOMENICO) Lettere fcritte dalla Sicilia, e dalla Turchia. In Firenze, 1779—1781, 12mo. IV tom. VIII tom.

The fame tranflated into German. Leipzig, 1780—1783, 8vo. *III Th.*

SCHIANO (DOM.) Defcrizione di varie produzioni naturali della Sicilia. Palermo, 1762.

SWINBURNE (HENRY) travels in the Two Sicilies 1777—1780. London 1783, 1785, 4to. II vol.

The fame translated into French. A Paris, 1785, 8vo. tom. I.

Do. into German, with notes by Forſter, Hamburg, 1787, 8vo. *II Th.*

VERYARD, *vide* FRANCE.

Voyage

Voyage Pittoresque, *vide* NAPLES,
WELSCHEN, *vide* ARCHIPELAGO.

SIERRA MORENA.

Befchreibung einer Reife, welche in die Sierra Morena im Jahr 1769, von Elfas aus unternommen wurde. Leipz. 1780, 8vo.

SILESIA.

ANDROPHILI, *vide* FRANCONIA.
AUSTEL in HACKLUYT, *vide* ANGLESEY.
BUQUOI, Reifebefchreibung durch einen Theil des Schlefifchen Geburges. Bunzlau, 1783, 8vo.
------- Fortfetzung. Bunzlau, 1784, 1785.
FRID. WILHELM II Reife von Berlin zur Huldigung Schlefiens nach Breflau, 1786, 8vo.
HAMMOND (C. F. E.) Reife durch Ober Schlefien nach der Ukrain. Gotha, 1787, 8vo. 1ter Band.
TROSCHEL, *vide* BERLIN.
Von Schlefien vor und nach dem Jahr 1740, Freyburg, 1785, 8vo. II Th.

SIMENTHAL.

LANGHANS (DAN.) Merkwürdigkeiten des Simenthals im Bernifchen. Zurch, 1753, 8vo.

SLEWICK.

HERMANNIDAE deliciae, *vide* FINLAND.
ZEILLER, *vide* DENMARK.

SPAIN.

AUNOY (COMTESSE DE) Relation du voyage d'Efpagne. A Amfterdam, 1716, 12mo. III tom.
The fame tranflated into German. Leipzig, 1695, 12mo. III Th. Nordhaufen, 1782, 8vo. III Th.
Do. into *Englifh.* 1697, 12mo. III vol.
Do. into Dutch. Delft, 1705, 4to.
BARETTI, *vide* ENGLAND.
BERNOULLI's Archiv, *vide* BELLUNO.
Befondere Denkwürdigkeiten des heutigen Zuftandes der Monarchie von Spanien. Frankf. und Leipz. 1767, 8vo.
BEYRLIN, *vide* GERMANY.

BOISEL

Boisel, Journal d'un voyage d' Espagne fait en 1659. A Paris, 1722, gr. 12mo.

Bosii Hisp. *vide* Milan.

Bowles (D. Guil.) introducion a la historia natural, y geografia fisica del reyno de España. En Madrid, 1775, 8vo.

The same translated into French. A Paris, 1776, gr. 8vo.

Do. into Italian. In Parma, 1783, 8vo.

Breval, *vide* Alsace.

Brome, *vide* Italy.

Burge, *vide* Portugal.

Campomanes (D. Pedro Rodric) Itinerario de las carreras de posta por España. En Madrid, 1761, 8vo.

Cavanillas (D. Ant. Jos.) Observations sur l' article d' Espagne dans la nouvelle Encyclopedie. A Paris, 1784, gr. 8vo.

The same translated into German, with additions by Biester. Berlin 1785, 8vo.

Clarke (Edw) Letters concerning the Spanish nation. London, 1763, gr. 4to.

The same translated into German. Lemgo, 1765, 8vo.

Colmenar, *vide* Portugal.

Crome, *vide* Europe.

Coulon (Louis) Fidele conducteur pour le voyage d' Espagne. A Paris, 1754, 8vo.

Dalrymple, *vide* Portugal.

Der

Der Schauplatz, *vide* PORTUGAL.

Des Königreichs Spanien Land—Staats—und Städte Beschreibung. Leipzig, 1700, 12mo.

DILLON's (JOHN TALBOT) travels through Spain. London, 1780, 4to. w. C.
Tranflated into German, and encreafed by J. A. Engelbrecht. Leipzig, 1782, gr. 8vo. II Th.

DRAKE in HAKLUYT, *vide* ANGLESEY.

EBERT, *vide* ENGLAND.

EICHHOFII (CYPRIANI) deliciae Hifpaniae, &c. Urfellis, 1604, 4to.

ENS (CASP) Deliciae apodemicae. Coloniae, 1609, 8vo.

ESCRIVANO (JOS. MATH) itinerario Efpañol. En Madrid, 1758, 12mo.

GOES (DAMIANI A) De rebus Æthiopicis, Indicis, et Hifpanicis opufcula. Colon. 1574, 8vo.

HAKLUYT, *vide* ANGLESEY.

HERVEY, *vide* GERMANY.

HILL, *vide* FRANCE.

JAMES's (THOMAS) Hiftory of the Herculean ftraits, now called the ftraits of Gibraltar. London, 1771, 4to.

JOSTEN, *vide* AUSTRIA.

KAIMO (Norb) Lettere d'un vago Italiano nel 1755

1755, &c. In Pitburgo, 1759, 1767, 8vo. II tom.

The fame translated into French. A Paris, 12mo. *II tom.*

Ditto into German. Leipz. 1774, gr. 8vo.

LABAT, *vide* ITALY.

LAET, *vide* PORTUGAL.

LANGLE (MARQUIS DE) Voyage de Figaro en Espagne. A Neufchatel, 1785, 8vo. II tom.

The fame tranflated into German. Leipzig, 1785, 8vo. *II Th.*

LOEFLINGII (PET.) iter Hifpanicum eller refa til Spanfka länderna uti Europa, och America, förrätad ifräm 1751 til 1756.

The fame tranflated into German, by Kvelpin. Berlin, 1776. gr. 8vo.

Letters from an Englifh traveller in Spain in 1778, on the origin and progrefs of poetry of that kingdom, &c. &c. London, 1781, 8vo.

LIMBERG VEL RODEN, *vide* ENGLAND.

LUTZENKIRCHEN, *vide* FRANCE.

M. voyages faits, *vide* FRANCE.

M. Lettres fur le voyage d' Efpagne. A Pampelune, 1756, 12mo.

MASCARENAS (HIER) Viaje de la Reyna Doña Anna de Auftria en Efpaña. En Madrid, 1650, 4to.

MONCONYS, *vide* CONSTANTINOPLE.

NAVAGERO, *vide* FRANCE.

Neuere Staatſkunde von Spanien. Berlin, und Stettin. gr. 8vo.

NEUMAYR VON RAMSLA, *vide* ITALY.

P. (.) Eſſai ſur l'Eſpagne, &c. A Geneve, 1780, 8vo. & ſous le titre: Nouveau voyage en Eſpagne. A Londres, 1782, 8vo. II tom.

The ſame translated into German. Leipzig, 1781, gr. 8vo. II Th.

P. **, Voyage d'Eſpagne curieux, hiſtorique, & politique fait en 1655. A Cologne, 1667, 12mo.

The ſame tranſlated into Dutch. Amſterd. 1669, 8vo.

PLUER'S (CARL. CHRIST.) Reiſen durch Spanien. Leipzig. 1777, 8vo.

PUENTE (PED. ANT. DE LA) Viaje de Eſpaña. En Madrid, 1776—1786, 8vo. XIII tom.

—————— (PONZ.) Reiſe durch Spanien, mit Erläuterungen und Zuſätzen von Dietz. Leipz. 1775, 8vo. II Th.

RAY, *vide* FRANCE.

Reiſebeſchreibung nach Spanien, *vide* ENGLAND.

Reiſebeſchreibung nach Spanien. Frankfurt, 1676, 8vo.

Reiſbeſchryving, *vide* ENGLAND.

Relation d'un voyage d'Eſpagne. A Paris, 1664, 12mo. A Cologne, 1667, 12mo.

Remarques d'un voyageur fur la Hollande, *vide* GERMANY.

RESENDII deliciae, *vide* PORTUGAL.

RODEN *vide* ENGLAND.

ROSMITAL, *vide* do.

S. voyage de France, *vide* FRANCE.

Sammlung der beften und neueften Reifebefchreibungen, *vide* CYPRUS.

SALAZAR (A. DE) Inventaire general des plus curieufes recherches des royaumes d'Efpagne, traduit de l'Efpagnol par lui même. A Paris, 1612, 1615, 8vo.

SCHEID, *vide* ENGLAND.

SINCERI, *vide* PORTUGAL.

SPOERL's vermifchte Briefe, *vide* HOLLAND.

SPRENGEL, *vide* ENGLAND.

SWINBURNE's (HENRY, travels through Spain. London, 1779, gr. 4to. w. c.

THICKNESSE, *vide* CATALONIA.

TORRUBIA (JOSEPH) apparato para la hiftoria natural Efpánola. En Madrid, 1754, fol. II tom.

The fame tranflated into German, with notes Murr. Hall, 1773. gr. 4to.

TWISS, *vide* PORTUGAL.

UDAL AP RHYS, *vide* do.

VAL, *vide* do.

VAYRAC (ABBE DE) Etat prefent de l' Efpagne. A Amft. 1719, 8vo, 3 tom.

VERYARD, vide FRANCE.
Versuch über die Staatsverfassung, &c. von Spanien. Hamburg und Kiel, 1783, gr. 8vo.
Viaje de España. En Madrid, 1776, 12mo. VI vol.
VOLKMANN's neueste Reisen durch Spanien vorzüglich in Ansehung der Kunst, Handlung, Oeconomie, und Manufacturen. Leipzig, 1785, gr. 8vo. II Th.
Voyages faits, vide GERMANY.
WELSCHEN, vide ARCHIPELAGO.
ZEILLERI itinerarium, vide PORTUGAL.

S P A W.

BERNOULLI, vide AUSTRIA.
SPRINGSFELD (GOTTL. CARL) iter medicum ad Thermas Aquisgranenses, & fontes Spadianos. Lipsiae, 1748, 8vo.

S P I R E.

BERNOULLI, vide AUSTRIA.

SPITSBERGEN.

KUEHN, vide CANARY ISLANDS.
MARTEN, vide GREENLAND.

Roy (P. L. le) Relation des avantures arrivées à quatre matelots Ruſſiens jettés ſur une iſle deſerte prés d'Oſt-Spitzbergue, 1766, 8vo.
The ſame translated into German. Riga und Mietau, 1768, 8vo.
ZORGDRAGER vide GREENLAND.

STAFFORDSHIRE.

ERDESWICK (S.) Natural hiſtory of Staffordſhire. Oxford, 1686. fol.
PLOT's (ROB.) natural hiſtory of Staffordſhire. Oxford, 1679, Do. 1686, fol.

STIRIA.

ARNOLD's Reiſe in Steyermark. Wienn, 1785, 4to. m. 1. K.
BROWN, vide AUSTRIA.
CHURELICHZ, vide CARNIOLA.
FERBER, vide HUNGARY.
HERMANN, vide AUSTRIA.

STIRLINGSHIRE.

NIMMO's (WILL) general and natural hiſtory of

of Stirlingshire. Edinburgh, 1777, 8vo. London, 1778, 8vo.

STOCKHOLM.

BREDERODE, *vide* LUBECK.
WRAXAL, *vide* COPENHAGEN.

STRAIT DAVIS.

ANDERSON, *vide* GREENLAND.
KUEHN, *vide* CANARY ISLANDS.
ZORGDRAGER, *vide* GREENLAND.

STRASBURGH.

A descriptive journey, *vide* FRANCE.
BERNOULLI, *vide* AUSTRIA.
Neue Reisebemerkungen, *vide* BERLIN.
SHERLOCK, *vide* Do.

SURREY.

AUBRY's (JOHN) natural history and antiquities of the county of Surrey. London, 1720, 8vo. V vol.
SALMON's (NIC.) antiquities of Surrey, &c. London, 1736, 8vo.

SUSSEX.

BLUGDEN's (RICH) Survey of the county of Suffex. London, 1756, 8vo.

SWABIA.

BERNOULLI, *vide* AUSTRIA.
CASSINI DE THURY, *vide* Do.
GERKEN, *vide* BAVARIA.
HUINLIN's (DAVID) Staats und Erdbefchreibung des Schwäbifchen Kreifes. Ulm, 1780, 1781, gr. 8vo. II Th.
Reife eines Curländers durch Schwaben, &c. Ulm, 1784, 8vo.
SULZER, *vide* ALSACE.
WEKHERLIN, *vide* AUSTRIA.
ZAPF, *vide* BAVARIA.
-------- Über die Abficht meiner litterarifchen Reife in einige Klöfter Schwabens, und der Schweitz. Augfb. 1781, gr. 8vo.
-------- Über meine vollbrachte Reife in einige Klöfter Schwabens und in der Schweitz. Augfb. 1782, gr. 8vo.

SWEDEN.

ACRELIUS (ISRAEL) Beschrifning om de Swenska Församlingers första och nawarande tilst and uti niefwerige. Stockholm, 1759, 4to.

ADAM, *vide* DENMARK.

An account of Sweden, 1694, 8vo.

Translated into Dutch. Gravenhaag, 1695, 8vo.

AUBERY DE MAURIER, *vide* DENMARK.

BERNOULLI's archiv, *vide* BELLUNO.

‒ ‒ ‒ ‒ ‒ ‒ ‒ Fortgesezte Sammlung im 14ten Band, *vide* AUSTRIA.

BUESCH (JOH. GEORG.) Bemerkungen auf einer Reise durch einen Theil Schwedens im Jahr 1780. Hamburgh, 1783, gr. 8vo.

CANZLER (JOH. GEORG.) Memoires pour servir á la connoissance des affaires politiques & economiques du Royaume de Suede. A Londres, 1776, 8vo. II vol.

The same translated into German, with additions. Dresden, 1778, 8vo. II Th.

CARLISLE, *vide* DENMARK.

COX, *vide* Do.

GOETCERI, *vide* Do.

HAER-

HAERLEMANN (CARL.) Dagbok öfwer en ifran Stockholm, igenom åtſkillige rikets landſkaper gjörd rcſa. Stockholm, 1749, 1751, 8vo. II del med kopp.
The ſame tranſlated into German. Leipzig, 1751, 1764, 8vo. II Th.
HEBERER VON BRETTEN, *vide* DENMARK.
HERMANNIDAE DELICIAE, *vide* FINLAND.
HILL VEL MARSHALL, *vide* DENMARK.
JARS, *vide* ENGLAND.
Journal van het geſandſchap, *vide* POLAND.
LEOPOLD (JO. FRID.) Relatio epiſtolica de itinere ſuo Suecico 1707 faƈto ad J. Woodward. London 1720, 8vo.
LETTRES GALANTES, *vide* ENGLAND.
LINNAEI OLANSKA, *vide* GOTHLAND.
------- Skanſka reſa förrättet ao. 1749. Stockholm, 1751.
------- Reiſen durch einige Schwediſche Provintzen überſetzt durch Schreber. Hall, 1764, 1765, 8vo. II Th.
--------- Reiſen durch das Königreich Schweden überſetzt mit Anmerkungen von Klein. Leipzig, 1756, 8vo.
LOMENII ITINERARIUM, *vide* AUSTRIA.
MAGNI, *vide* NORTHERN COUNTRIES.
MAGNUS (OL.) Hiſtory of the Goths, Swedes, and Vandals, 1658. fol.
MOTRAYE, *vide* CRIM.

NEGRI (FRANC) Viaggio in Suecia. Padua, 1706, 8vo.
OCERII EPHEMERIDES, *vide* DENMARK.
OWEXIONIUS, *vide* FINLAND.
PAYEN, *vide* BRABANT.
PRAETORII orbis GOTHICUS, *vide* GOTH-LAND.
REGNARD, *vide* DENMARK.
SCHEEL, *vide* do.
TUNELD's (ERIC) Geographie öfwer Konungariket Swerige, &c. Stockholm, 1786, 8vo.
RUDBECK, *vide* ALAND.
Viaggio d'un uomo, *vide* ENGLAND.
WILLIAMS, *vide* DENMARK.
ZEILLER, *vide* FINLAND.

SWITZERLAND.

AFSPRUNG's, *vide* APPENZELL.
ALBON (GRAF VON) *vide* EUROPE.
ALTMANN (JOH. GEORG . Verfuch einer hiftorifchen und phyficalifchen Befchreibung der Helvetifchen Eifberge. Zurch, 1751, 1753, 8vo.
Andreae (J. G. REINH.) Briefe aus der Schweitz. Zurch und Winterthur, 1776, gr. 4to.
BERNOULLI, Lettres fur differens fujets, *vide* FRANCE.

Do.

Do. *vide* AUSTRIA.

BESSON, manuel pour les favans & les curieux, qui voyagent en Suisse. A Bern, 1786, 8vo. II tom.

BESSONI's mineralogische Reise und Beobachtungen uber die Gebürge der Schweitz: Aus dem Französischen überfetzt. Bern, 1782, 8vo.

BJOERNSTAEHL, *vide* CONSTANTINOPLE.

BLAINVILLE, *vide* do.

BOURRIT, *vide* ALPS.

BOYLE, *vide* FRANCE.

BREVAL, *vide* ALSACE.

BURDE, *vide* ITALY.

BURNET, *vide* FRANCE.

Briefe eines Sachfen, *vide* LEIPZIG.

Briefe einer reifenden Dame aus der Schweitz, Frankf. und Leipzig, 1786, 1787, 8vo.

COXE's (WILL.) Sketches of the natural, civil, and political state of Switzerland. London, 1779, 1780. gr. 8vo.

The fame translated into German. Zurch, 1781, gr. 8vo.

Do. *into French.* A Paris, 1780, 8vo.

COXE's (M. W.) Lettres fur l'état politique civil, & naturel de la Suisse. A Paris & Laufanne, 1787, 12mo. II tom.

D*** voyage hiftorique, *vide* GERMANY.

DANNEBUCHI (ARMINIO) relazione del paese

de' Svizzeri e loro alleati. In Venezia, 1708, 8vo.

Dictionnaire geographique, hiftorique, & politique de la Suiffe. Nouvelle edition corrigée & augmentée avec la grande carte de la Suiffe de Rob. de Vaugondi. A Geneve & Laufanne, 1776, 8vo. II tom.

GERKEN, *vide* BAVARIA.

-------- *vide* SWABIA.

GRASSERI ITINERARIUM, *vide* ITALY.

GRUNER (GOTTL. SIGM.) Eifberge des Schweitzerlandes. Bern, 1760, 8vo. III tom.

The fame tranflated into French, by M. Keralio. A Paris, 1770, *gr. .4to.*

-------- Naturgefchichte Helvetiens in der alten Welt. Bern, 1757, gr. 8vo.

GUALANDRIS, *vide* ENGLAND.

HALLERI (ALB.) iter Helveticum anni 1739, & iter Hercynium anni 1738. Götting. 1740, 4to.

Handbuch für Reifende durch die Schweitz. Bern, 1777, 8vo. II Th.

HEIDEGGERI differtatio de peregrinationibus religiofis, *vide* COMPOSTELLA.

HIRSCHFELD (CHRIST. CAJUS LORENZ) Briefe die Schweitz betreffend. Leipzig, 1776, 8vo.

-------- Neûe Briefe über die Schweitz. Kiel 1785, 8vo. 1ter Heft, m. VII Kart.

Hifto-

Hiſtoriſche, geographiſche, und phyſicaliſche Beſchreibung des Schweitzerlandes

KEYSSLER, *vide* BOHEMIA.

LABORDE (DE) & ZURLANDEN (BAR. DE) tableaux topographiques, pittoreſques, hiſtoriques, moraux, politiques, litteraires de la Suiſſe. A Paris, 1777, 1780, gr. fol. tom I.

L' étaɩ & les delices de la Suiſſe en forme de relation critique par pluſieurs auteurs celebres. A Leide, 1714, 12mo. IV tom. A Paris, 1776, 12mo. IV tom.

Lettres ſur la Suiſſe. A Paris, 1783, 8vo. II tom.

LUC (J. A. DE) Lettres ſur les montagnes de la Suiſſe. A la Haye, 1778, 8vo.

M ( ) Reflexions on Dr. Burnet's travels, *vide* FRANCE.

M. (C. D. S.) *vide* ALSACE.

M. (C. P. D.) *vide* ENGLAND.

MAYER (DE) voyage en Suiſſe en 1784, 1786, 8vo. I tom.

MEINERS (CHRISTOPH.) Briefe über die Schweitz. Berlin, 1784, 1785, gr. 8vo. 2 Th.

MEISTERS (LEONH.) Kleine Reiſen durch einige Schweitzer Cantons. Baſil, 1782, 8vo.

Merkwürdige Proſpecte auf den Schweitzer Gebürgen

Gebürgen &c. Bern 1776, gr. fol. mit
10 illum. Kupfern.

MONTAGNE (MICH. DE) *vide* ITALY.

The *fame tranflated into German*. Hall, 1777,
8vo.

MOORE, *vide* FRANCE.

MALLERI (CHRIST. HENR.) itineris fui in Helvetiam facti commentarii, Fridericoftadii, 1769, 4to.

NERINI (F. M.) Iter Subalpinum. Francof. &
Lips. 1754, 8vo.

NICOLAI, (FRID.) *vide* GERMANY.

OEDER, *vide* ENGLAND.

PATIN, *vide* BOHEMIA.

PILATI, *vide* EUROPE.

PLATIERE, *vide* ITALY.

POCOCKE, *vide* ARCHIPELAGO.

RANDOLF, *vide* DENMARK.

R*** (DE LA) voyage d'un amateur, *vide*
FLANDERS.

REBOULET, & BRUN (LA) Voyage de Suiffe,
en 12 lettres. A la Haye, 1686, 16mo. II
part.

Reifen durch die merkwürdigften Gegenden
Helvetiens. London, 1778, II Th.

Reife eines Officiers, *vide* ITALY.

Reifen in verfchiedene Länder von Europa,
vide EUROPE.

ROCHE (FRAU VON LA) Tagebuch einer
Reife

Reife durch die Schweitz. Altenburg, 1787, 8vo.

RODEN VEL LIMBERG, *vide* ENGLAND.

ROUCHAT (GOTTL. DE) fous le nom de (G.) KYPSELEN: Etat & delices de Suiffe, &c. A Amft. 1730, gr. 12mo. 4 tom. A Neufchatel, 1778, 4to.

------- Uber das intereffantefte aus der Schweitz. Aus dem Französifchen überfetzt, befichtiget, und vermehrt von Ulrich. Leipzig, 1777—1778, 12mo. IV Th.

SALTZMANN's Bicftafche, *vide* FRANCE.

SCHEUCHZERI hiftoriae naturalis Helvetiae prolegomena, Tigur. 1700, 4to.

- - - - itineris Alpini defcriptio. Lugd. Bat, 1723.

The fame tranflated into German. Zurch. 1718, 4to. III Th. *Do.* 1746, 4to. II Th.

SCHEUCHZER's (JOH. JAC.) Befchreibung der Elementen, Grentzen, und Bergen des Schweitzerlandes, 1ter. Th. Zurch, 1716.

- - - - Befchreibung der Seen, Flüffen, Brunnen, warmen und kalten Bädern, und andern mineral Wäffern des Schweitzerlandes, 2ter. Th. der Naturgefchicht des Schweitzerlandes. Zurch, 1717, 4to.

- - - - Befchreibung der Luft-gefchichten, Metallen, und Mineralien, abfonderlich auch

der

der Uberbleibfeln der Sündfluth, der 3ter Th. Zurch, 1718, 4to.

SCHINTZ (HANS) Beyträge zur nähern kenntnüfs des Schweitzerlandes. Zurch, 1783, 8vo.

SCHINTZ (SALOMON) Differtationes phyficae de itineribus per Helvetiam cum fructu faciendis. Tigur, 1782, 1783, 4to.

SINNERS (DE) Voyage hiftorique & littéraire de la Suiffe Occidentale. A Neufchatel, 1782, 8vo. II tom.

The fame translated into German. Leipzg, 1782, 8vo. II Bände

STANIAN's (ABR) Account of Swifferland written in 1714. Edinb. 1756, 8vo.

-------- (AMBASSADEUR D' ANGLETERRE) Etàt de la Suiffe. A Amfterdam, 1714, 8vo.

SULZER, *vide* ALSACE.

-------- Befchreibung der Merkwürdigkeiten, die er in einer 1742 gemachten Reife durch einige Oerter des Schweitzerlandes beobachtet hat. Zurch, 1743, 4to.

SULZER, *vide* EUROPE.

Viatorium Germaniae, *vide* GERMANY.

Voyage hiftorique de Suiffe, *vide* Do.

WAGNERI (JOH. JAC) Hiftoria naturalis Helvetiae curiofa. Tiguri. 1680. 12mo.

------ Mercurius Helveticus fürftellend die

Denck

dènck—fchauwürdigften Sachen und Sel-
tenhetein der Eidgenoffenchaft. Zurch,
1701, 12mo.
WITTENBACH (JOH. SAM) Beyträge zur Na-
turgefchichte des Schweitzerlandes, &c.
Bern, 1775, gr. 8vo. 1 Band, 2 ftuck.
ZAPF, vide BAVARIA.
Do. vide SWABIA
ZURLANDEN & LABORDE, vide Supra LA-
BORDE.

TARTARY.

AVRIL, vide EUROPE.
Befchreibung einer Reife eines Polnifchen
Bothfchafters, vide CONSTANTINOPLE.
BERGERON (PIERRE) Relation des voyages en
Tartarie de (Guil) de Rubriqueis (Jean de)
Plan Carpin, (Fr.) Afcelin (a 1246) & au-
tres religieux, &c. A Paris, 1734, 8vo.
BRONIOVII defcriptio, vide MOLDAVIA
BRUCE, vide GERMANY.
BRUSSII (GUIL) diarium de Tartaris. Colo-
niae, 1595, fol.
CHROMER, vide HUNGARY.
COOK, vide RUSSIA.
HAKLUYT, vide ANGLESEY.
HERBERSTEIN, vide RUSSIA.
KLEEMANN, vide ARCHIPELAGO.
MOTRAYE, vide CRIM,

Neuefter

Neuester Staat von Cafan; Aftracan, Georgien, und vielen andern dem Czaaren, Sultan, und Schah zinsbahren und unterthanen Tartarn, Landschaften, und Provintzen. Nurnberg, 1723, 8vo.

OLEARIUS, *vide* RUSSIA.

PAULUS VENETUS (MARCUS) de regionibus. Accedit Haithoni Arameni historia orientatis, quae & de Tartaris inscribitur. Itemque Mülleri (And) de Chataja disquisitio. Colon, Brandenb. 1671. 4to.

The same translated into Dutch. *Amsterdam*, 1664, 4to.

Do. into German, (by Hier. Megissero.) Leipzig, 1611, 8vo. *m. K.*

QUIR (FRANC. FERD.) Narratio de Terra Auftrali incognita, & de terra Samojedarum, &c. in Tartaria. Amst. 1613, 4to.

Recueil de divers voyages curieux en Tartarie, &c. A Leide, 1729, 4to. II vol.

RUSSIA ITEMQUE TARTARIA, *vide* RUSSIA.

SCHILDBERG's, Gefangenschaft in der Turkey. Frankf. 1557, 4to.

Staat der gesammten Tartarey in den alten und neuen bewährtesten Zeiten aus den bewährtesten Nachrichten gezogen. Reval und Leipzig, 1780, 8vo.

STRAHLENBERG, *vide* RUSSIA.

STRUYS, *vide* GREECE.

THE-

THEVENOT (N. M. DE) Relation de divers voyages curieux. A Paris, 1696, fol. IV part.
TOTT, vide CONSTANTINOPLE.
ULFELDI LEGATIO, vide RUSSIA.
VEER, vide NORWAY.
WITSEN's (NIC.) Noord en Oost Tartarye, Amsterdam, 1705, fol. II deel.

TEMESWAR.

BORN (IGNATZ. VON) vide HUNGARY.
GRISELINI, vide CARINTHIA.
SULZER, vide ALSACE.

TENERIFFE.

KINDERSLEY's (MISS) letters from the island of Teneriffe, &c. London, 1777.
The same translated into German, Leipz. 1777, 8vo.

THESSALY.

BROWN, vide AUSTRIA.

THRACIA.

BLOUNT, vide DALMATIA.

POCOCKE, *vide* ARCHIPELAGO.

TIROL.

BREVAL, *vide* ALSACE.
HACQUET's (B.) mineralogisch-botanische Reise von dem Berge Terglou in Krain zu dem Berge Glockner in Tirol, im Jahre 1779 und 1781. Wien, 1784, 8vo. m. IV K.
HERMANN, *vide* AUSTRIA.
WALCHER's (Jos.) Nachrichten von den Eisbergen in Tirol. Wienn und Leipz. 1773. 8vo.

TRANSYLVANIA.

BENKOE (JOSEPH) Transylvania. Viennae 1778. Tom. I. & II.
BORN, *vide* HUNGARY.
FRANCISCI (T.) Dissertatio de memorabilibus Transylvaniae. Witteb. 1690, 4to.
LEHMAN (Jos.) *vide* HERMANSTADT.
POSSEVINII MOSCOVIA, *vide* RUSSIA.
SULZER, *vide* ALSACE.

TRIESTE.

GRISELINI, *vide* CARINTHIA.
KLEEMANN, *vide* ARCHIPELAGO.

TURIN.

ADLER, vide AMSTERDAM.

TURKEY.

Aulae Turcicae Othomannicique imperii descriptio. Bafil, 1573, 8vo.

BJOERNSTAEHL, vide CONSTANTINOPLE.

BRUINING VON BUCHENBACH, Reife in die Turkey, in Europa fowohl, als Afia und Africa. Strafburg, 1712, fol.

BRUCE, vide GERMANY.

BUSBEQUII (AUGERII GISLENII) Legationis Turcicae epiftolae. Antwerp, 1595, 8vo. Monachii. 1620, 8vo. Leipzig, 1688, 12mo.
Tranflated into German. Franckf. 1696, 8vo.
Do. into Englifh. London, 1694, 8vo. 1741, 8vo.
Tranflated into French. A Paris, 1748, 12mo. *III tom.*

CHISHULL, voyage into Turkey. London, 1747.

BUSSINELLO's (PET.) Hiftorifche Nachrichten von der Regierungs-Art, den Sitten und

Ge-

Gewohnheiten der Ottomannifchen Monarchie. Leipzig, 1778, 8vo.

CLENARDI epiftola de rebus Muhammeticis. Lovanii, 1551, 8vo. Hanov. 1606, 8vo.

CROIX (DE LA) Memoires concernant diverfes relations trés curieufes de l' Empire Ottoman, A.Paris, 1684, 8vo. II vol.

Die Reifen des Orients. Aus dem Engl. Wurtzburg, 1779, fol.

DRIESCHII (GERH. CORN) Hiftoria magnae legationis Caefareae, quam Caroli VI aufpiciis fufcepit Comes Damianus Hugo Virmontius ad Portam Othomannicam. Viennae, 1721, 8vo.

The fame tranflated into German. Nurnberg, 1723, gr. 4to.

Epiftolae duae, quarum altera de moribus ac inftitutis Turcarum agit, altera feptem Afiae ecclefiarum notitiam continet. Oxon. 1672, 12mo.

FEBURE (MICH.) Etat prefent de la Turquie. A Paris, 1675, 8vo.

FLORI, Navigazioni e viaggi nella Turchia. Anveras, 1576, 4to.

GALLAND, Recueil des rits, & ceremonies du pelerinage de la Mecque, auquel on a joint divers ecrits relatifs a la religion, aux fciences, & aux moeurs des Turcs.

A Paris

A Paris, 1754, 12mo. A Amsterdam, 1754, 12mo.

Translated into German. Nurnberg, 1757, 8vo.

GEMELLI CARRERI, *vide* BARCELONA.

GIORGIEWITZ ( ) De Turcarum moribus Lugd, 1555, 12mo. Genev. 1598, 16mo.

GUER ( ) Moeurs & usages des Turcs, leur religion, leur gouvernement civil, militaire, & politique. A Amsterdam, 1747, 4to. II tom.

GUYS, *vide* GREECE.

HACKLUYT, *vide* ANGLESEY.

HABESCI (ELIAS) Present state of the Ottoman Empire, from the French manuscript. London, 1784, 8vo.

Translated into German. Lubeck, 1785, 8vo.

HILL (AARON) Full and just account of the present state of the Ottoman Empire in all its branches. London, 1735, fol.

------- A general history of the Ottoman empire. London, 1740, fol.

Histoire critique de la creance & des coûtumes des nations du Levant, publiée par le Sr. de Mont. A Frankf. 1684, 12mo.

HOPPELII thesaurus exoticorum, *vide* HUNGARY.

JOSTEN, *vide* AUSTRIA.

Libellus de ritu & moribus Turcarum ante LXX annos editus: Cum praefatione M. Lutheri. Witteb. 1550. 8vo.

LUCAS

Lucas, vide Greece.

Luedecke (Christ Wilh) Glaubwürdige Nachrichten von dem Türkifchen Reich. Leipz, 1770, 8vo.

------- Do. unter dem Titel: Befchreibung des Türkifchen Reichs nach feiner Religions und Staats Verfaffung in der letzten Hälfte des 18ten Jahrhunderts. Leipzig, 1780, 8vo.

Magni (Corn) Viaggio per la Turchia nei anni 1672, 1673. Bologna, 1685, 12mo.

------ Quanto di piu curiofo e vago ha potuto raccorre nel primo bienno 1672, 1673. Bologna, 1685, 12mo.

Melton (Ed) Zee en land reifen door Egypten, Turkien, &c, 1660—1667. Amfter. 1681, 4to.

Menairno (Geo. Ant) i coftumi, e la vita de' Turchi, con nna prophetia, ed altre cofe Turchefche tradotte per (Lud) Domenichi. In Firenze, 1551, 8vo.

Mont (du) vide France.

Montalbanus (Jo. Bapt) De moribus Turcarum. Romae, 1636, 8vo.

Motraye, vide Crim.

Nicolai (Nic de) Difcours & hiftoire veritable des navigations, peregrinations, & voyages faits en Turquie en 1550. A Anvers, 1586, 4to.

Tanflated

Translated into German, Nurnberg, 1572, *fol.*
Do into Italian. In Venez. 1580, *fol.*
Obfervations on the religion, laws, government,
and manners of the Turks. London,
1768, 12mo.
OTTER ( ) Voyage en Turquie. A Paris,
1748, gr. 12mo, II vol.
The fame tranflated into German. Nurnberg,
1781, *gr.* 8vo. *Iter Th.*
PEREGRINI (B. G.) De Turcarum moribus epi-
tome. Lugd. Bat. 1552, 12mo.
PICZERI (Jo) De Turcarum moribus libellus.
Hanover, 1686, 12mo.
PORTER's obfervations on the religion, law,
government and manners of the Turks.
London, 1768, 12mo. II vol.
The fame tranflated into French. by Bergier,
A Neufchatel, 1770, 12mo.
Do. into German. Leipzig, 1768, 8vo.
R. (D. L.) Memoires contenants fes voyages
en Turquie. A la Haye, 1749, 12mo.
RICAUT's (PAUL) Hiftory of the prefent ftate of
the Ottoman empire. London, 1689, 8vo.
The fame tranflated into French, by Priot. A Pa-
ris, 1670, 4to. *Do.* 1671, 12mo. II tom.
Do. by Pefpier. A Rouen, 1677, 12mo. II
tom.
Do. into Dutch. Amft. 1670, 4to.
Do. into Italian, In Bologne, 1674, 12mo. *Do.*
in Venezia, 1677, 4to.

L l   Do.

D. imTheatro Europco. Do. in der eröfneten Ottomannifchen Pforte. Augfb, 1694, 4to.

Roque (de la) Memoires contenans des voyages en Turquie. A la Haye, 1754, 12mo. II vol.

Rosaccio (Gius) Viaggio da Venezia a Conftantinopoli per mare, e per terra, &c. In Venezia, 1598, 4to.

Sandy, vide Greece.

Sapienza. vide Constantinople.

Saviour Lusignan tranflated from the Englifh. Leipzig, 1784, 8vo.

Schildberger, vide Tartary.

Schmid's (N.) Funfjährige Gefangenfchaft unter den Turken. Drefden, 1635, 4to.

Seidel, vide Constantinople.

Sestini, vide Sicilia.

Smithii (Thom) De moribus ac inftitutis Turcarum. Oxonii, 1674, 8vo.

Sommer's, vide Archipelago.

Spandigino (Theod.) Origine e coftumi de Turchi. In Firenz. 1551, 8vo.

Stoeveri (Joh. Herm.) Hiftorifch ftatiftifche Befchreibung des Ofmannifchen Reichs. Hamb. 1784, 8vo.

Strasburgii (Paul) Relatio de Byzantino, itinere, as negotiis in Ottomannica aula peractis; 1633, 4to.

Strwys,

STRUYS, *vide* GREECE.
Tableau de l' empire Ottoman. A Frankf. 1757.
TAFFERNER (PAUL) Ambaffade à la porte Ottomanne ordonnée par L' Empereur Leopold I. A Vienne, 1672 12mo.
TAVERNIER (JEAN BAPT.) Six voyages en Turquie, &c. A Paris, 1724, 12mo. VI vol.
The fame tranflated into German. Nurnberg, 1681, *fol. III Th. Cenf.* 1781, *fol. III Th.*
Do. into Englifh. London, fol.
Do. into Italian. In Roma, 1682, 4to. *II vol.*
THOMPSON's travels, *vide* FRANCE.
TOTT, *vide* CONSTANTINOPLE.
Tractatus de Turcis. Norimb. 1481, 4to.
Tractatus de ritu, ac moribus Turcarum. Leipz. 1488, 4to.
Tractatus de moribus & inftitutis fpurciffimis Turcarum, &c. 1514, 4to.
Turken Chronicke, Glaube, Gefetze & Sitten, von einem Siebenbürger. Zwickau, 1530 4to.
VALLE (PIET. DELLA) Viaggi in Turchia, &c. In Roma, 1663, 4to. IV tom.
The fame translated into French. A Paris, 1661 4to. *IV tom. Do. a Amft.* 1665, 8vo. *VIII tom.*
Do. into Dutch, A Amfterd. 1665, 4to. *VI deel.*
Do. into German. Genf. 1674, fol. IV Th.

Voyage d' un miſſionaire de la Compagnie de Jeſus en Turquie, &c. A Paris, 1730.

TUSCANY.

A ſhort account of a late journey to Tuſcany, Rome, and other parts of Italy. London, 1741, 8vo.

TARGIONI TOZETTI (GIO. ANT.) Relazioni d' alcuni viaggi fatti in diverſe parti della Toſcana per oſſervare le produzioni naturali, e gli antichi monumenti di eſſa. In Firenze, 1751, 1754, 8vo. XII tom.

    Ediz. II con copioſe giunte. Do. 1768, 1779, 8vo. XII, om. c. f.

— — — — Prodromo della corografia e della topografia fiſica della Toſcana. In Firenze, 1754, 8vo.

UKRAINE.

BARDILI, *vide* GERMANY.
BEAUPLAN, *vide* CRIM.
HAMMARD, *vide* SILESIA.
MARSHALL vel HILL, *vide* DENMARK.

UPLAND.

RUDBECK, vide ANGERMANLAND.

VALLENGIN.

BERNOULLI's ( ) Sammlung kurtzer Reisebeschreibungen, &c. Berlin, 1783, 8vo.
BERTRAND, vide NEUFCHATEL.
OSTERWALD, vide Do.

VELAI.

FAUJAS de St. FOND, vide LANGUEDOC.

VENICE.

ADLER, vide AMSTERDAM.
BARBARO, vide ITALY.
BELLIN, vide MOREA.
COTONII (JOAN) itinerarium Hierosolimitanum & Syriacum anno 1598, accessit synopsis reipublicae Venetae. Ant, 1619, 4to.
GRISELINI, vide CARINTHIA.
PIRKS ( ) Itinerarium per ditionem Venetorum, 8vo.

Ro-

ROSACCIO, *vide* TURKEY.

STRIDBECKS (JOH) Curiofer Reifegefährte von Augsburg nach Venedig. In Charten, Abriffen und Tabellen. Augfb. 4to.

Viaggj d'un uomo qualificato, *vide* ENGLAND.

VERSAILLES.

SAUGRAIN, *vide* St. CLOUD.

VESUVIUS.

BULIFON (ANT.) Compendio iftorico del monte Vefuvio. Napoli, 1698, 8vo.

COLINI (COSMUS) Betrachtungen über die Vulcanifchen Berge nebft einer Tabelle über die Geburge, Drefden. 1783, 4to,

GIULIANI (GIO. BER) Trattato del monte Vefuvio, e de' fuoi incendj. In Napoli. 1732, 4to.

HAMILTON (SIR WM.) *vide* ÆTNA MOUNT.

----- Supplement to the Campi Phlegraei: being an account of the great eruption of Mount Vefuvius of Auguft, 1779.

Hiftoire du mont Vefuve avec l'explication des phenomenes qui ont coûtume d'accompagner les embrafemens de cette montagne. A Paris, 1741, 8vo.

ME-

MECATTI (GIUS MARIA) Racconto iftorico-filofofico del Vefuvio. In Napoli, 1754, 4to.

PARAGALIO (GASP) Iftoria naturale del Monte Vefuvio divifa in due libri. In Napoli, 1705, 4to.

Phyficalifche Briefe uber den Vefuv, und die Gegend von Neapolis. Leipzig, 1785, 8vo.

QUIÑONES (JUAN DE) El monte Vefuvio. Madrid 1632, 4to.

SORRETINI (IGN) iftoria del Vefuvio. In Roma, 1734.

TORRE (GIOV. MARIA DE LA) Storia e fenomeni del Vefuvio. In Napoli, 1755, 1768, 4to.

The fame tranflated into French. A Paris, 1776, 8vo.

Do. into German, with Additions, by Lentin. Altenburg, 1783, gr. 8vo.

VETRANI (ANT.) Prodromo Vefuviano, &c. in cui oltre al nome, origine, antichità, prima fermentazione, ed eruzione del Vefuvio fi propongono le cautele da ufarfi in tempo degli incendj, &c. In Napoli, 1780, 8vo.

VIENNA.

ADLER, *vide* AMSTERDAM.
BERNOULLI's Sammlung 13ter und 14ter Band, *vide* AUSTRIA.
BURNEY, *vide* BOHEMIA.
DINI (JOSEPH) Vollſtändiges Tagebuch von der Reiſe Pius VI nach Wienn. Breſlau, 1783, 8vo.
FABRI, *vide* FRANCE.
GOTSCHED (JOH. CHRIST.) Singularia Vindobonenſia. Lips. 1756, 4to.
GUSTA (FRANC.) Viaggi de Papi; aggiuntovi un ragguaglio del viaggio del regnante Pio VI a Vienna. In Firenze, 1782, 8vo.
KLEEMANN, *vide* ARCHIPELAGO.
NICOLAI (FRID.) Beſchreibung einer Reiſe, &c. Berlin, 1784, 3ter und 4ter Th.
Reiſe von Wienn, *vide* BERLIN.
SEIDEL, *vide* CONSTANTINOPLE.
SHERLOCK, *vide* BERLIN.
TOLLII, *vide* BERLIN.

WALLACHIA.

BAUER (DE) Memoires hiſtoriques & geographiques de la Valachie avec un proſpectus d'un atlas geographique & militaire de la derniere

derniere guerre entre la Ruffic & la porte Ottomanne. Frankf. 1778, 8vo.

GARRA, *vide* MOLDAVIA.

SULZER, *vide* Do.

WALES.

BERNOULLI, *vide* AUSTRIA.

BROME, *vide* ENGLAND.

CHILDREY, *vide* Do.

CRADOCK's account of fome of the moft romantic parts of North Wales. London, 1777, 8vo.

Defcription of all the counties, *vide* ENGLAND.

England illuftrated, *vide* Do.

GIRALDI (SYLV.) Itinerarium Cambriae, feu laboriofae Balduini Centauri Archiepifcopi per Walliam legationis anno 1188 factae accurata defcriptio; cum annotationibus D. Powell. London 1585, 8vo.

MARTIN, *vide* ENGLAND.

MOLL, *vide* Do.

Obfervations made during a tour, *vide* Do.

PENNANT's (THOM.) tour in Wales. London, 1778, 1783, gr. 4to. II vol.

ROGER, *vide* ENGLAND.

SULIVAN, *vide* EDINBURGH.

The modern univerfal Britifh traveller, *vide* ENGLAND.

A month's tour in Wales, *vide* DUBLIN.
WYNHAM's (HENRY PENRUDDOKE) tour through Monmouthshire and Wales. London, 1781, 4to.
YOUNG, *vide* ENGLAND.

WARWICKSHIRE.

DUGDALE's antiquities of Warwickshire. London, 1656, fol.
Sketch of a tour, *vide* BEDFORDSHIRE.

WATERFORD.

SMITH's (C.) ancient and present state of the county of Waterford. Dublin, 1746, 4to.

WAYGAT's STRAITS.

HACKLUYT, *vide* ANGLESEY.
Verhaal van de eerste Scheepvaart door Waygats, t' Amsterd. 1650, 4to.

WEIMAR.

Neue Reisebemerkungen, *vide* BERLIN.
Tagebuch einer Reise, *vide* GOTHA.
VOIGT (I. C. W.) Mineralogische Reisen durch

das

das Hertzogthum Weimar und Eisenach, Dessau. 1782, 8vo. I Th.
WILL, *vide* ALTDORF.

WESTMORELAND.

EHRENMALM's Reise durch Westmoreland in der Bibliothek der neuesten Reisebeschreibungen. Frankf. & Leipz. 1780, 1782, 8vo. V Bande.
NICOLSON, *vide* CUMBERLAND.
ROBISON, *vide* Do.

WESTPHALIA.

BERNOULLI, *vide* AUSTRIA.
Neue Reisebemerkungen in und über Deutschland, *vide* BERLIN.
Tagebuch einer Reise, *vide* GOTHA

WIGHT (ISLE OF)

STURCH's (JOHN) view of the Island of Wight, London, 1778, 8vo.
The same translated into German. Leipz. 1781, 8vo.
WORSLEY's history of the Island of Wight, London, 1781, 4to.

WURTEMBERG.

Casini de Thury. *vide* Austria;
Wekherlin, *vide* Do.

YORKSHIRE.

A tour to the caves in the environs of Ingleborough, &c. London, 1780, 8vo.

YVIÇA.

Campbell, *vide* Formentera.

ZANTE.

Dapper, *vide* Cefalonia.

ZURCH, LAKE OF

Escher (Joh. Erh) Beschreibung des Zurcher See. Zurch, 1692, 8vo.

APPENDIX,

TO THE

LIST OF WORKS,

INTENDED FOR

The Inſtruction and Benefit of Travellers.

BROWAL (J) de emolumento ex itinere per provincias patriae inſtituto. Aboae, 1749, 4to.

GOETZII (GEORG. HENR) ecloga de peregrinationibus eruditionis Orientalis cauſa ſuſceptis. Lubec, 1716, 4to.

KOEHLER (JOH. DAV.) Anweiſung für reiſende Gelehrte, Bibliotheken, Müntz Cabinetten, Naturalien, und andere Sammlungen mit Nutzen zu beſehen. Frankf. und Leipzig, 1762, 8vo,

SA (JOSE ANT. DE) compendio de obſervaçoens, que formão o plano da viagem politica e filoſofica, que ſe deve fazer dentro da patria. Liſboa, 1783, 8vo. III tom.

Yorurtheile der Deutſchen bey Antretung ihrer Reiſe in aufwärtige Länder.

APPENDIX,

TO THE

EUROPEAN TRAVELS.

ARCHIPELAGO.

Boschini (Marco) Arcipelago con tutte le ifole, fcoglj, fechi, e baffi fondi, &c. In Venezia, 1658, 4to.

AUSTRIA.

M. (C. F.) Anmerkungen über die natürliche Befchaffenheit der Kais. Königl. Erbländer. Augfb. 1763, 8vo.

BANNAT of TEMESWAR.

Griselini (F.) Verfuch einer politifchen und natürlichen Gefchichte des Temefwarer Bannats. Wienn. 1780, 4to. II Th.

BURGUNDY.

BEQUILLET, defcription generale & particuliere du duché de Bourgogne. A Dijon, 1775, 8vo.

DENMARK.

RAUPACH (BERN) de utilitate peregrinationis Daniae. Kilon. 1712. 4to.

ENGLAND.

BLANC's (LE) Letters of the French and English nations, London, 1747, 8vo.
BOCCAGE (MAD. DE) Lettres, vide ENGLAND. *This work is also tranflated into Englifh.* London, 1770, 8vo. II vol.
Do. into German. Drefden, 1776, 8vo.

FLANDERS.

PAYEN, vide BRABANT.
POCOCKE vide ARCHIPELAGO.

FRIES-

FRIESLAND.

SIOERD (FOCKE) hiftorifche jaerboeken van
Oud & Nieuw Friefland. Leward, 1769.

GERMANY.

ENS DELICIAE GERMANIAE. COLON, 1612,
8vo.
SYLVII (AENEAE) de ritu, fitu, moribus, &
conditione Teutoniae defcriptio. Lips.
1496, 4to.

GREENLAND.

KUEHN, *vide* CANARY ISLANDS.

HUNGARY.

B. (DU) Lettres fur les Hongrois. Amft. 1748,
8vo.

ITALY.

EICHHOFII (CYP.) Deliciae Italiae. Urfellis,
1603, 4to.

EISLINGS

EISLING (CHRISTOPH.) Breviarium itineris
Italiac. Norimb. 1664, 4to.
ELVERI DELICIAE, *vide* ENGLAND.
MAGINI (GIOV, ANT.) L' Italia defcritta. In
Bologna. 1620, fol.

MINORCA.

PASSERAT (CL. FR.) reflexions generales fur l'
ifle de Minorque, fon climat, la maniere de
vivre de fes habitants, & les maladies, qui
y regnent. A Paris, 1764, 8vo.

NETHERLANDS.

HOEN, *vide* ENGLAND.

NORTH SEA.

MULLER, *vide* ICY SEA.

NORWAY.

HERMANNIDAE, *vide* DENMARK.
HOLK (H.) Norfk vegvifer for veyfende. Kiobenh 1774, 12mo.

PONTOPPIDAN, *vide* NORWAY.
The same translated into German by Scheiben. Ko-
penh. 1754, 8vo. II Th.
Do. into *English.* London, 1755, fol.

R O M E.

FRIDERI (J.) Feriae Viadrinae. Stettin, 1652, 8vo.

R U S S I A.

HAVEN (PEHR) Reise til Rusland. Ciop. 1744.
-------- Nye og forbedrede efderrätninger om det Russiske Rige. Ciop. 1747, 8vo. II Deelen.
-------- Reise in Rusland, nebst einem Anhang. Copenh. 1744, 8vo.

S A X O N Y.

Essais d' economie politique, &c. A Bâle, 1786, 4to,
Do. translated into German. Leipzig, 1786, 4to.

SCOTLAND.

PENNANT, *vide* HEBRIDES.

SWITZERLAND.

M.** Lettres ecrites de Suiſſe, *vide* ITALY.

TUSCANY.

TOZETTI's (D. J. T.) Reiſen durch verſchie-
dene Gegenden, von Toſcana, in einem
Aufzug von Iagemann. Leipz. 1787, 8vo.
II Th.

www.ingramcontent.com/pod-product-compliance
Lightning Source LLC
Chambersburg PA
CBHW032051230426
43672CB00009B/1553